Let's Kill All The Lawyers

The Third Anthony Firestone Thriller

By Jessica Schluff

I0514250

To my dad; a man who always gets to the truth plus he *called dibs* on it

Copyright 2018-03-04

All rights reserved by the author

Jessica Schluff

PART ONE – JUDGE, JURY, AND EXECUTION

Chapter 1

People rarely wake up expecting that the day ahead of them is going to be their last day alive; being correct in that expectation is even rarer still, but such was the case for successful but fragile-minded divorce attorney, Lawrence Daily.

Right from the first second his eyes opened that morning; Daily couldn't shake the feeling of impending doom. He fought to warm the icy fingers of terror creeping up and down his neck as he dressed in his favorite cream suit and packed his papers into his brown attaché case before walking to work.

Fear's icy fingers were beating his mind in the battle for supremacy over his focus as Daily walked the crosswalk between his apartment building and the law firm where he worked.

He was so distracted by his shivers that he failed to notice a cab driver, too busy texting to see the crosswalk, almost run him down.

The cab bumped Daily's knee and both men jolted to life quickly enough to prevent the accident from going any further. Daily jumped out of the way and narrowly kept his attaché case from flying, the cabbie apologized, and Daily made it to his office without another incident, but, even in the safety of his office, Daily still felt threatened. Daily wondered if his fears were because his first appointment of the day was with such a dangerous client.

Daily, Stevens, and Associates Family Law Firm was Washington D.C.'s foremost law firm for divorces and custody disputes. They catered to the rich, the famous, and the politically affluent. Daily, obviously, was the lead founding partner.

Daily's office had an ultra-modern style. It had slick mat-black furnishings and a captivating city skyline view out a gigantic picture window. Three walls and the door were frosted glass, but the back wall, crowning the window, was rich red wood with reclaimed redwood shelving. The shelves were stocked with awards and framed photos of Daily shaking hands with movie stars and previous presidents.

Daily was running his palm lovingly over his desk and chair as he admired his awards and his view. He was moving like a man about to leave the place that he loved to never see it again when his secretary came in.

"Mr. Daily, Mr. Brenner is..." She paused suddenly. She could see that he was startled and tearful; *in the middle of a goodbye.* "Are you alright, sir?" She asked.

Daily pulled himself together quickly. "Yes, of course; what was that you were saying about Brenner?"

"He's here, sir."

Daily took a heavy breath, "Send him in then."

Before Daily knew it, he was explaining that he intended to discontinue representing Landon Brenner, to Brenner. Brenner wasn't the easiest man to walk away from.

Landon Brenner looked out of place in the ultra-modern and deafeningly calm office. Brenner wore tattered blue jeans, an obscure rock and roll T-shirt, a second-hand black leather jacket, dark sunglasses, and fingerless gloves.

Brenner's hair looked like oily chocolate swirls instead of the groomed quaff of a man of his influence and he had an awkwardly trimmed beard that fit his aging-rocker image, but he wasn't a rock star.

Brenner was the sole designer, creator, and CEO of social media site, Family Page. Family Page was a website that helped people trace their ancestry, build their family tree, and connect with their relatives. More recently, it had also branched off into Family Builder: an online dating service for the rich and prominent.

His success meant that Brenner had more money than all of Daily's other clients combined. As far as Daily was concerned, Brenner could have come in wrapped in brown paper and wearing a tin foil hat and still qualify as a client; Brenner's image wasn't the issue. The real problem was that Brenner was as wild as he looked. Brenner was dangerously unstable and had recently broken the law; Daily no longer wanted to be tied to such a magnet for trouble.

Daily was a good foot shorter than Brenner and he was plump. He was not a fighter. He was a well-dressed and well-off older gentleman with a level of physical and emotional sophistication that matched his position at such a traditional firm, but he tried to make himself appear more intimidating by propping his elbows up on his massive stained-black mahogany desktop. He then tented his fingers in a domineering pyramid as he spoke steadily.

"I'm sorry, Mr. Brenner, but our firm handles family matters exclusively. Divorce and custody matters are things I can handle, but I'm afraid that as soon as you broke into your wife's house and destroyed those paintings and those cars, your case became a criminal matter. I can't help you now."

Brenner started fidgeting like an addict looking for a fix. "You're a lawyer, aren't you?"

At first, he spoke in a nervous near-whisper, but Brenner's words gained volume and strength as he continued. "I mean, law school is law school, right?"

"I'm sorry, Mr. Brenner, but your treatment of your soon-to-be-ex-wife has reached a criminal level and our firm does not associate with criminals. Not only can I not help you, but I also don't want to."

Brenner suddenly stood and began using overzealous hand gestures, in addition to becoming even louder with every word. "I don't understand; that house was mine, those cars were mine, and those paintings were mine. I can't be charged for going into my own house and my own garage or for wrecking my own property inside, right?" By his final sentence, Brenner had come behind Daily and started whispering in Daily's ear.

For the duration of Brenner's visit, Daily had done a convincing job of being calm and settled behind his domineering desk, but Brenner's growing instability and tightening proximity were becoming increasingly unsettling. The uncomfortable pressure of impending doom had returned with a vengeance.

Daily's eyes drifted to his attaché case and, for a brief moment, he strongly considered scooping it up and leaving, but instead, he simply let a nervous cough escape his lips and flattened his hands on the desktop. As much as every nerve in his body protested, he remained otherwise immoveable in a desperate effort to stay in control of the failing situation.

Daily lowered his own voice and spoke slowly, choosing each word carefully in another effort to calm Brenner down, "Mr. Brenner, you're forgetting that we already signed the house over to your wife and because the garage is attached to the house, she owns it too. Because she owns the house and the garage, she has an immediate right to everything inside the house and the garage. When you entered the property without her permission and destroyed those paintings and cars you broke the law and now, because you broke the law, you now need to get the legal matters dealt with before your divorce proceedings can continue and I cannot help you in criminal court."

Daily tried to hand Brenner a stapled stack of papers. He explained, "This is a comprehensive list of names of competent criminal attorneys I'm personally familiar with. They can help you, but while you're working with them, there is no point in keeping me on retainer... I'm trying to save you money here..."

Brenner had stepped back a bit, but hadn't calmed down any. He slapped the list to floor, shouting, "You sit there with your well-groomed white hair, expensive cream suit, and college championship rings on those plump manicured fingers pretending that you care about what happens me, but you don't give a damn, do you?"

Brenner was really yelling now. "That wrist watch you're wearing must cost as much as some cars and I probably paid for it..." Brenner then pulled Daily out of his chair and started backing Daily into a corner. Daily's body made quite a noise when it contacted the wall. Various pictures and knick-knacks that were shelved were sent crashing to the floor.

"You're not trying to save anything, are you?" Brenner accused loudly, "Not my money and not me; you're just trying to suck more money out of me and you're trying to use one of your criminal law buddies to cover your ass."

"What's the plan here, bub? You take your retainer for a while and then once I destroy or give up too many of my assets, you fix it so one of your friends has to help me in criminal court, then you guys split what he makes off me 50-50 before you step back in and 'finish' my divorce, huh? Is that what this is?"

"Mr. Brenner, please," Daily had become terrified and was now begging for space and mercy. Fortunately, his door flew open and Daily's secretary came in. Secretary Rhonda Wheatly was a small blonde mouse of a woman, but she was smart enough to bring two bulky security guards with her when she came to Daily's rescue.

As the security guards began to drag Brenner away, he shouted, "My wife was right: you lawyers are all just money-mongrels. Every dirty thing that's ever been said about lawyers is true; you're proof of that and you'll pay for it."

As soon as Brenner was out of sight, Daily moved to stare out his office's window which, in addition to its breathtaking skyline view, also overlooked the firm's parking lot.

Wheatly could see that Daily had become emotional, so she asked again, "Are you alright, sir?"

Daily did not answer until they both saw Brenner's black convertible sports car tear out of the lot. "I am now." Daily said.

From the distance away that they were, Daily and Wheatly did not see Brenner take several swigs of the cheap tequila he kept in his glove box before placing a call to his wife.

Daily didn't know it yet, but Brenner's drinking and phone call doomed them both.

Daily was a zombie for the remaining six hours of his work day. He barely managed to roll through the motions and complete his other meetings and file work. Ms. Rhonda Wheatly was too smart and caring to let her boss go home in the fog he was in so, as everyone was about to leave for the day, she rallied Daily's partner, Drake Stevens, and a few others from around the office for drinks at

Crooks Bar: the small pub less than a block away from their firm.

At first, Daily bucked the idea of socializing, but as soon as he walked into Crooks Bar, his mood immediately adjusted.

Crooks Bar had teal walls that were decorated with local artwork and combination wood and metal shelving packed with modern and antique liquors. Crooks offered cheap drinks, loud live local music, and the best pub food in the city.

Tonight, a local band with a teenage girl singer was performing their acoustic renditions of 1920's jazz. With its smiling staff and hopping atmosphere, Crooks Bar could stitch up even the most broken of people.

During dinner, Daily went from near-death to being overjoyed. For the first time that day, the cloud of coming death had lifted. Unfortunately, those feelings of joy and freedom were only the calm before the storm that was his end.

By the time the group finished dinner and drinks, it was approximately 9:30pm and dark. The street outside Crooks was quiet until a car roared to life from behind everyone and out of their sight.

Initially, everyone thought the approaching car was just a bar employee heading home. They continued to wrap up their conversations and say their goodnights, making enough noise that they didn't notice the car bump over the curb and drive towards them on the sidewalk.

Before anyone truly understood what was going on, the intruding car slammed into the group. In that single incomprehensible instant, Daily died.

Daily's secretary, Rhonda Wheatly, was safely sealed in her car when the accident erupted. She saw the black convertible sports car run down and kill Daily and his partner Stevens. Two of the younger partners and another secretary were injured as they sent tumbling over the car, but because they were tossed over it instead of being crushed and sliced by the undercarriage, they survived.

Although the convertible top was up, Rhonda Wheatly recognized the car immediately. It was a black sports car and its plate was BRNR. It was definitely Landon Brenner's car. The accident damaged the vehicle enough to cause the interior lights to flash on off unpredictably. Thanks to those interior lights, Wheatly could swear she saw a dark haired woman driving...

Wheatly called for help. Ambulances and police responded immediately.

A burly officer named Ron Michaels approached Wheatly and when he spoke to her, showed no compassion for her; he simply asked the obvious, "What happened here?"

Wheatly's entire world was suddenly crushed under the spinning of some sporty car tires, so it was no surprise that her initial statement was fragmented and foggy.

"Um, I saw the car… It was Landon Brenner's car. Black sport convertible with a plate reading BRNR." Wheatly huffed. She then turned and started stumbling away from Officer Michaels. As she stumbled, she continued to mutter, "I knew the Brenner was angry and Daily feared his anger, but would he do this? *No; a woman was driving…*"

Michaels heard every word Wheatly muttered, but what Wheatly didn't know was that Officer Michaels already knew who was driving. He didn't care about the woman. *He wanted to place Landon Brenner behind that wheel.*

"You said you recognized the car as Landon Brenner's and that this Brenner was angry. Tell me more..." Just then a sudden gust of wind scattered the contents of Daily's ravaged attaché case.

Those scattered papers, when composed, comprised a very incriminating file on Landon Brenner. Apparently, Daily intended to leak some government suspicions to the tabloids. Apparently, Family Page was fronting identity theft from its supremely wealthy clientele. The file also showcased intimate details of the Brenners' volatile relationship, making Brenner appear like a real-life monster. More importantly to the police was the fact that Daily's file listed all of Brenner's addresses.

Michaels felt he had what he needed and he convinced the other police officers to race to Brenner's bachelor penthouse.

Brenner's interior decorating style was as punk-rock as his clothing choices, but after strategically searching every messy room and closet, they found that Brenner was not there.

Sarah Brenner, Brenner's stunningly beautiful and dark haired future ex-wife, already knew where Landon was because she had placed him there. She also knew that because he'd gone there before, the police would be coming to her house expecting to find him. It was her job to ensure that the police left her alone and found Landon where she placed him.

She drove his car into Daily and his grouping of staff. She then lured Landon out to a secluded park where she'd dumped his car, so the police would believe that he was the driver, but the accident had left her badly battered. She worried that the police would take one look at her injuries and recognize her guilt.

To soften her concerns, she telephoned a friend within the police service, "I don't have a lot of time; officers will be at my door any minute." Sarah frantically explained, "I've done my part and I'm making sure that you remember our deal. Everything's set on my end to make certain Landon goes to jail instead of me; how about your end?"

The remarkably calm feminine voice of her friend said, "Just point us to the park and Landon's doomed, leaving you his fortune, or at least, whatever's left of his fortune after I get my half that you promised me. How's that going to work by the way?"

"You're the one that told me that it was finances that doomed Amilio Scarleto after that firestorm, remember? You're just going to have to trust me the way I'm trusting you now. A year from now, we'll both be rich beyond our wildest dreams."

"A lot can change in a year..."

"Trust me, damn it." As she shouted, Sarah heard multiple vehicles pull up. She pushed her curtains aside with her fingertips to unveil a cluster of police cars clouding her driveway. "They're here. *We're trusting each other now, right?*"

"Absolutely." Her partner said.

Upon them entering the Brenner mansion, a battered Sarah Brenner met the officers on her grand staircase. She immediately preformed an Oscar-worthy damsel in distress act.

"Officers, I was just on the phone with someone from your service to try and get help; has Landon confessed to trying to kill me? Have you come for my statement?"

All of the officers, except Michaels, looked at one another in shock. No one, except Sarah, noticed Michaels' lack of emotion. Michaels nodded slightly but comfortably at Sarah's moonstruck expression and, after a moment, one of the officers said, "Um, no ma'am. It appears as though your husband is involved in a murderous accident; we need to question him. Have you seen him?"

Sarah cried convincingly, "He came here at about three this afternoon." She sobbed and stumbled her way into one of the officer's arms. "He was drunk and spouting on and on about how our divorce was a mistake. He blamed his lawyer, Lawrence Daily, for basically everything that's ever gone wrong in his life, especially the breakdown of our marriage and then, he proposed to me again."

She sniffled and wiped her tears away before she continued talking and started to pace the room. "Naturally, I refused and we fought." She stopped pacing and stared the officers down, "I really thought he was going to kill me and then he suddenly stopped beating me and asked if things would be different if Daily was dead."

Sarah was lying. Landon had only called her after he'd been removed from Daily's office. He did cast a lot of blame on Daily and he did propose a second time, but Landon's outlining his argument with Daily created an opportunity to delicious for her to resist.

She refused his proposal and used a beating as an explanation for her injuries as she framed him for murder.

The officers shared another look and she knew that she had them hooked. To be certain of Landon's doom, she put a cherry on top, "Before I could do anything to stop him, he ran out muttering: *before daybreak, all of our problems will be solved* and he said..." she began to whimper, "That he'd be waiting for me at the park where he first proposed, in case I changed my mind..."

Based on her words, the police raced to the park and found Brenner soaking wet, drunk, and passed out on the park bench overlooking a swan pond. His black sports car was submerged in the pond up to its rear wheels.

Officer Ron Michaels was very heavyset and was aging quickly. Michaels was famous for his unapproachable attitude and numerous excessive force complaints. It was rare to see him smile, but as he watched Landon Brenner get packed in a police car, he smiled wider than actor in a commercial for toothpaste.

The other uniformed officers and forensics processors studied Michaels with mixed feelings as they watched him happily call his boss on his cell phone. He made sure to talk loudly to give everyone an opportunity to interject a correction, but he already knew that no one would object to what he had to say; *most of the people processing the scene with him were in on the framing of Landon Brenner.*

"It appears as though Landon Brenner went out drinking after being tossed out of Daily's law office." Michaels explained. "Once drunk, it appears that he attacked his ex-wife and, when she rejected him, he went on a killing spree before retreating to a place that made him happy. We found him at the park where his wife said he'd be; the murder car's here too."

Michaels paused while the same feminine voice that Sarah had spoken to questioned him. "Is our case solid?"

Michaels resumed, "Well, it looks like the pond water washed away any blood evidence, but some hairs from what I assume are the people that had been driven over are still entangled in the rumpled metal of the damaged hood, so yeah, he's already in the car. We've got this one in the bag..."

For Brenner the wheels of justice turned remarkably quickly. Six weeks after the car accident,

Brenner was on trial for the property damage that brought him to Daily's office, two counts of vehicular homicide, six counts of attempted murder for those staffers who were either hit or traumatized but not killed, and the assault on his wife.

Chapter 2

It was the day that the Brenner Trial was set to begin, six weeks after Daily's fatal accident, and former FBI Special Agent Anthony Firestone and his wife, Leah Fong-Firestone, were up very early that morning.

A massive rainstorm had struck the previous night and their small house was in the middle of being renovated; meaning the roof was opened up and sheets of construction plastic were all that lay between the storm clouds and their partially renovated interior.

For hours, the Firestone's had been scrambling for towels and buckets to minimize the damage of the leakage from those plastic sheets.

The cold truth was that the Firestone's five-year marriage was in a state of crumbling, but between their panic and their fatigue, this particular morning was especially difficult.

Leah was usually a quiet, composed, and high-fashion Chinese beauty, but since her wedding, she had grown too thin and cut her hair down to a bob that was much too short for her face. Her looks were at least partly the result of post traumatic stress left over from the shooting that took their status as FBI agents into the former.

Today, her hair was static-ridden, her pajamas were mismatched, and she was damp from the mess she was trying to clean up.

Eventually, she gave up and, slapping her latest soaked towel to the floor, shouted, "Tony, I asked you to hire a separate roofing company. I knew the guys we hired to do our whole-home renovation were spreading themselves much too thin and they were never going to get the roof done before the rain. Now look at this place! Not only will we have to have these cabinets re-primed, but these floors..." Leah failed to finish her sentence and cried.

As she yelled, a defeated Anthony Firestone had kept trying to dry the kitchen floor, but as Leah's anger turned to tears, he slowly dropped everything and wrapped his arms around her.

Anthony was 51 years old, approximately six-foot-three, and bordering on being overweight at 230 pounds. Leah was ten years younger than Firestone. She was nearly a foot and half shorter and she only weighed about 100 pounds these days.

As Firestone held her, he found himself reflecting, not for the first time, on how different they were. When their relationship first began, they were both muscular accomplished federal agents with star-powered smiles. Their minds always seemed to be on the same wavelength as they worked together to catch criminals and sparred together at the gym between cases to keep fit and fired up.

Then they were both in the same shooting. In the seven years since their shooting, both of them lost their badges and some of their star-power, but Leah seemed to have lost more than he had.

After the shooting, he and Leah worked through two years of therapy before marrying. Then, post-honeymoon, Leah became a lawyer. She had graduated from law school before joining the FBI and Anthony had always suspected that she regretted becoming an agent instead of lawyer. He always suspected she stayed on to work with him, but Leah had a big brother with an established law firm and a place for them both and, post-shooting, they couldn't physically be agents any longer, so he felt it was his turn to work with her.

Anthony became a private investigator at Leah and her brother's divorce law Firm: Daniel Fong and Associates. Firestone knew that being a private investigator would mean trading in the high-octane and medal worthy action of the FBI for sleazy photographs of cheating spouses taken between vending machine snacks, but he signed on because the job paid well and the fun and freedom of working for family was a perk he could not pass up. He had made his peace with his past and his future, but Leah hadn't. He had adjusted while Leah aged, cried, and blamed everything, including her unhappiness and the damage of this recent rainstorm, on him.

Apparently, being a lawyer wasn't what she always dreamed and it wasn't helping her heal.

In days passed, Firestone tried to help her, but everything he tried seemed to hurt her more and, as more and more cracks developed in their relationship, the differences between them became greater.

His struggles with her hardened him. He had more or less stopped putting in the effort of helping her and he began noticing things like the fact that his eyes were bluer while hers were dark. Her hair was black his was grey. She was young and he wasn't. She felt like a child in his arms and not the love of his life.

He knew he should have felt love coming from both her and his own hearts as they embraced, but all he felt was the resignation of neither of them wanting to be there anymore.

"Leah," he said carefully, "We've been at each other's throats since we bought this fixer upper. I think we both thought that a shared project would take us back to our roots of being partners again, but I think we're doing something wrong..."

Without leaving his embrace, Leah assessed the room and whispered, "Yeah, I have to agree."

"Let's just go to a hotel for some rest and relaxation today. We'll revisit our living situation after we've had a hot shower and a good night's sleep..."

Leah pushed him away and mumbled in frustration, "Anthony, I cannot miss work today. I've got people I need to see."

"Daniel is just going to have to understand and make alternate arrangements because we're not ourselves right now Lee."

Ultimately, Leah agreed and they packed up their belongings and settled into a hotel room.

In the hotel room, they showered *separately* and settled into a nap on the four-star fluffy bed, but after a meager hour of sleep Firestone awoke and stepped out into the hall so he could make some phone calls without disturbing Leah.

The first call he made was to their law firm to try and explain why they were absent.

"Hello Daniel, it's Anthony, I'm sorry, but neither Leah nor I will be in today. The rain we got last night flooded our house and we need to take steps to fix it and ourselves and we can't do what we need to do at work..."

Unfortunately, Leah's brother and their boss, Daniel Fong, was not a very understanding man. "That simply won't do, Anthony." Daniel said, "Leah has clients that need to see her *today* and I'm still waiting on the Sullivan, Donahue, and Smith files from you; their coming in today as well..."

Anthony cringed because that really wasn't what he *needed* to hear, but he said, "I understand. We'll both come in for the afternoon..."

Daniel gave a dissatisfied sigh, but Anthony's displeasure must've soaked through the phone line because Daniel allowed it. "I'll schedule your clients around that then..." Daniel then hung up abruptly.

Anthony Firestone's next call was to the construction company responsible for his home's renovation. Firestone called them to explain that their home had become uninhabitable due to the lack of forward progress with the renovation:

"I understand what my wife and I agreed to," He said, "And I understand that the weather is out of your control, but my wife and I are really unimpressed and now that we have to pay for hotel housing and repairs in addition to the original scope of work..."

"You expect a discount..." the construction foreman unapproachably spat.

Between his tiredness and the wounds left over from Daniels surliness, Firestone barely remained calm with the rude foreman, but he did. "We need to revisit the budget, yes, and I think we need to look at the timeline here. My wife and I are done with the dust and the noise and the entire project..."

The construction foreman cut him off with respectful words but a disrespectful tone, "I understand your frustration Mr. Firestone. Let me go over to the project and assess how we can change things..."

It was Firestone's turn to release a dissatisfied sigh and commit to the deal as Daniel had done for him. "OK, but do it today or my wife and I will be forced to take our project elsewhere..."

With that, Firestone hung up and narrowly avoided punching a hole in the wall. His authority seemed to be challenged at every turn today, but suddenly, he found himself staring down at a complimentary copy of the day's paper.

The headline advertised the start of a trial at a particularly famous courthouse:

BILLIONAIRE BRENNER FACES CHARGES

Suddenly, images of his glory days convicting suspects for the FBI filled his mind. Something inside him demanded that he be a spectator at that trial, so he dressed in a dark suit and left a note for Leah that explained where he'd gone and the calls he had made. He also set an alarm that would wake her with enough time to appropriately prepare herself and meet Daniel on time. Then he left, not realizing how far he'd actually be going.

Chapter 3

Courtroom number five of the courthouse was a cave of honey-oak. The vaulted ceilings were made of honey-oak slats topped with honey-oak beams. The judges, witness's, and court stenographer's seats were all honey-oak nests that resembled roman chancellor pyres.

There were honey-oak church-style pews for spectators to sit on and polished honey-oak floors. The only things breaking up the honey-oak were; the creamy marble wainscoting that ran from approximately halfway up the wall to the ceiling, the local, national, and international flags stationed on either side of the judge, a concrete statue of blind justice in the rightmost corner, and the classic FBI crest behind the judge's head.

The FBI crest held Firestone's gaze. That eagle with its wings outstretched wings against a background of red, white, and blue stars and stripes, and all crowned with the words *'In God We Trust'* brought everything back.

So many of his FBI memories were bittersweet; like that glow in a mother's eyes when a jury foreman reads 'guilty' and formally declares that her child's killer would face punishment. That glow offered the sweet sensation of winning a battle, but the bitterness of the bitter-sweetness of those memories came from the fact that the mother's child was still gone. Sometimes it seemed like nothing he did was ever enough.

Beneath that eagle, one phase of life ended and new phases replaced them. Men and women went from freedom to prison or from loss to recovery.

When he finally broke away from the crest, he suddenly found himself receiving the red carpet treatment. The security officers greeted him with smiles, handshakes, and shoulder slaps. The spectators on both sides of the courtroom whispered, cooed, and even snapped a few pictures of him as he settled into a seat in the second row back from the front on the defence side of the courthouse to watch the events of People vs. Landon Brenner.

As he noticed them all continue to watch him and whisper, he began to feel less like a private investigator and more like the hero he had once been.

Seven years ago, Firestone, together with his then-partner-now wife Leah Fong, FBI Cyber

Specialist Angelique Marceau, CSI Lab Specialist Dawson Sour, Detective Donna Sparks, and reporter Rebecca Whales; resolved a massive murder conspiracy of terrible proportions.

It all started when the city's epicenter of both business and pleasure, the Carlton Tower, was apparently attacked by terrorists. The supermall-slash-hotel-and-casino-resort tower fell after two explosive devices were planted within it by a group pretending to be radicals and calling themselves The Brotherhood For A Pure America.

The BFAPA, as the group eventually became known, was not a terrorist group; they were actually a hit squad, hired by infamous international mobster: Amilio Scarleto and the part-owner of the Carlton Tower.

The tower's part-owner asked the hit squad to prevent the sale of the Tower by killing the other part-owner and the other men participating in the halted sale, but the explosions killed and injured thousands and inadvertently created a super-virus that killed hundreds more not even in the tower; ultimately 422,083 people died.

The massive death-toll was Scarleto's plan, not the tower part-owners', so she turned on Scarleto and his team of contract killers.

Until she co-operated and confirmed Scarleto's involvement in the scheme, Firestone was not allowed to investigate Scarleto as fully as he had wished. The woman also verified that the BFAPA, who were still utilizing the media to keep the city panicked, were just pretenders, but her confirmations came too late.

Despite Firestone chasing down the entire group and that case resulting in a dramatic shooting at an airfield, Scarleto and those of his group that were not killed in the firestorm that followed their actions at the tower, escaped by private plane with Leah as a hostage.

Even before the Tower fell, Firestone and Scarleto had a long history of playing cat and mouse with one another. Firestone had been so successful over the years that by the time the Carlton Tower job came along, Scarleto no longer cared about the details of the job, the money, or who would be hurt.

Scarleto saw the false terrorist image he'd given his team as his way of fragmenting the city so he could rise from the proverbial ashes and rebuild his long-standing criminal empire that Firestone had ruined.

To stage his criminal re-build, Scarleto reached out to another infamous gangster named Jacko Chang. Chang's gang, the Golden Dragons, had ties to Scarleto's crumbling empire and they had resources Scarleto passionately wanted, but Jacko Chang ultimately refused to deal with Scarleto.

At the time Scarleto first reached out to Chang, Leah was working undercover within the Golden Dragons and she became Chang's girlfriend as part of that cover, so Scarleto presented Leah to Chang as a traitor. Scarleto had intended Leah's ensuing torture to be a peace offering to solidify his partnership with Chang and the Dragons, but what Scarleto didn't realize was that Chang had truly fallen in love with Leah during the time they had spent together when she was undercover.

When Firestone finally tracked Leah down, Firestone and Chang bonded over their mutual love for Leah and hatred for Scarleto and with additional help from Chang and the Dragons, Firestone and his team successfully stopped Scarleto for good, but the final takedown injured both Firestone and Leah badly enough to cause them to have to retire from the FBI and ultimately become the people different they were today. Jacko Chang and the rest of the Dragons were killed and the rest of Firestone's team splintered into different directions as they accepted promotions, private positions, and political esteem.

Thinking about Leah and those dark days years ago sent him back on the downward slope of the emotional rollercoaster he found himself on. His mind drifted to his shelf full of worthless medals and a pitiful pension that barely covered the payments on a two bedroom-one bathroom fixer-upper home where he lived with his wife that was still recovering from her torturous experience and growing more distant every day. They had no children which was something they both regretted...

His list of regrets was growing with each passing second but thankfully, the trial began and consumed his thoughts.

Judge Harmon was presiding. Harmon was almost 70, but his hair still looked more black than white. He wore thin, almost invisible, glasses and he had a thick, comb shaped, mustache.

Harmon was a cop's favorite, meaning that he had a habit of handing out maximum sentences and he did not bend to technicalities easily, but Harmon was basically all that the prosecution had going for them.

The defendant's lawyer was Fred Tanning. Fred Tanning's sharply dressed mature image, southern drawl, red hair, and freckled complexion were unmistakable.

Firestone remembered Tanning from his FBI days. Tanning was *the* premiere mob lawyer. Rumor was that if Tanning could not convince the jurors to rule in his favor with his case and showmanship, he would buy them off. To Firestone's recollection, Tanning had never lost a trial and Tanning's showmanship was in fine form that day, so this trial looked unlikely for being Tanning's first loss.

Firestone could see that the defendant, Landon Brenner, had been dressed for court by Tanning. Brenner kept running his hands along his hairline and jaw bones and he kept tugging at his suit; the tell-tale signs of a man that was missing bushier head of hair and who was not used to such finely tailored clothing, but trimming the defendant's image was only page one of Tanning's plan. Firestone was watching page two unfold at the front of the courtroom.

Before he knew it, hours, *plural,* had passed and Firestone was watching Tanning cross-examine the prosecution's first witness. The woman, named Rhonda Wheatly, was a small, blonde, secretarial type with big brown glasses. Firestone gathered, from hearing her testimony so far, that the woman was the secretary of Mr. Lawrence Daily: one of the victims Brenner was on trial for killing.

While the prosecutor questioned her, Wheatly seemed smart and sure of herself, but Tanning was slowly shredding her faith in both herself and her recollection of the events of the night in question.

"So, you recognized the car's make, model, and plate as Brenner's car, but was my client driving the car?" Tanning asked.

The lady stammered as she answered, "Officer Michaels already said he was soaked in the pond water..."

Firestone cringed for two reasons. First, Michaels was another name Firestone recognized from his law enforcement days. Ron Michaels was a fat, ugly, and lazy slob that had multiple disciplinary actions brought against him for jumping to the wrong conclusions. A lawyer like Tanning could easily tear apart anything that a disgrace to the uniform like Michaels put forward and second, Firestone recognized the tremor in the secretary's voice. It was a tremor that he'd heard a thousand times before; it always came before that fiery-haired cross-examining lawyer achieved a win.

"I didn't ask you what some other people said, miss. I asked you whether or not you saw the defendant behind the wheel that night?"

"It was so dark and everything happened so fast..."

"Yes or no?"

Wheatly crumbled under Tanning's pressure, "No; as a matter of fact, I thought..."

Firestone noticed the prosecutor shoot Wheatly a murderous stare, causing her to stop speaking mid-sentence.

"You thought what, Ms. Wheatly?" Tanning asked calmingly as he strategically stepped between the secretary's sightline and the prosecutor.

"I thought I saw *a woman* behind the wheel that night..."

The prosecutor suddenly screamed, "*Objection*: statement is different from the on scene report to police..."

The prosecutor's sudden outburst caused everyone to jump and a chorus of gasps erupted. Through the noise, Rhonda Wheatly yelled, "I told the police what I thought I saw that night, but I only saw the driver for half of a second. The person I saw had dark hair and Brenner had dark hair. I thought it was a feminine figure, but I could've been wrong. I trust the police to know who to arrest."

"Thank-you, Ms. Wheatly." Tanning said with a smirk.

Although her faith in police at the last part of her statement seemed to salvage the prosecution's case, hardly anyone was listening to it and Tanning knew it. The prosecutor could have redirected, but she would have just had Ms. Wheatly repeating herself and Tanning would not have allowed that, so Wheatly was dismissed.

The prosecutor then called Officer Ron Michaels to the stand.

Through a series of questions, Michaels got to explain the events of that night in a way that complemented his policing, but then, it was Tanning's turn to break that testimony down.

Tanning walked up slowly. "So, Officer Michaels, Ms. Brenner told you that her husband went to see her, attacked her, and then he conveniently told her that he could be found at the park where you arrested him, correct?"

"Yeah, that's correct..."

"What time did Mr. Brenner supposedly attack Ms. Brenner?"

"I don't know."

Firestone cringed and chuckled simultaneously. He cringed because Michaels' answer meant that Michaels had failed to establish a timeline. Timelines were key in criminal cases; the timeline often meant the difference between suspects having alibis or not having them. Firestone also laughed because failing to establish something as important as a timeline was classic for Michaels.

Tanning went on nonchalantly, "But you documented her injuries and verified that they were the result of the physical attack that Ms. Brenner claimed to have experienced at her husband's hands, didn't you?"

"We were looking for Landon Brenner for murders by car. What happened to Ms. Brenner seemed unimportant."

Tanning made a surprised face at the jury and spectators and a chorus of giggles and gasps erupted from the crowd. Firestone laughed harder, but he took steps to hide his laughter in case his celebrity was still drawing attention.

As the room quieted, Tanning resumed, "So you just took her word that she was attacked by the defendant? I personally think that establishing that a victim's injuries are the result of an assault is important when pressing assault charges, but I think that verifying Ms. Brenner's injuries were *not* the result of, say, the car accident that is at the center of this case, would be vitally important Officer Michaels; don't you agree?"

The entire courtroom erupted into another chorus of accusatory whispers and gasps. Prosecutor Debra Lang harped her objections, but Michaels ignored the noise.

Michaels proclaimed, "We found him where she said he would be. We had no reason not to believe her."

Tanning took a dramatic pause to allow the courtroom to calm down and make sure his words stuck in the juror's minds. As he spoke and appropriately paused, he pushed his lips into humorous yet condescending expressions as he paced the room. Tanning was working the room.

"Officer Michaels, are you aware that there are a lot of people with access to my client's car at any given time; including the murder night?"

"I was not." Michaels snarled.

Tanning walked back and picked up a file folder from his table. He held up the folder for everyone to see. "Officer Michaels I have, in my hand, a forensics report that suggests that someone approximately five-foot-five was behind the wheel of the murder car that night. The defendant is just over six foot; too tall to have been the driver..."

The gasps erupted again.

Prosecutor Debra Lang jumped up and shouted, "Objection, your honour; the prosecution has not seen this evidence..."

Firestone panned over the entire room. Harmon and Tanning were both stoic, Landon

Brenner was stunned, and Prosecutor Lang looked ready to kill.

The jury was composed of seven women and five men of all different cultural and societal backgrounds. Two of the women and two of the men looked like they were over forty, but the other jurors looked like they were under thirty.

Firestone figured that the jury was structured that way because the younger generation was who Brenner's online business ultimately catered too. Tanning probably believed that a younger jury would be more apt to see Brenner as a friend subconsciously and therefore rule in his favor. In Tanning's courtroom, every decision was a cunning chess move.

Right now the jurors were experiencing a range of emotions, but regardless of whether they were showing anxiety, surprise, anger, or glee; all the jurors were glued to Tanning's every word; Tanning had made all of the right moves so far.

Tanning said, "Your honor, this is an official police report. The prosecution should already have it. This is obviously a stalling tactic to cover the fact that their officer did not take a harder look at Ms.

Brenner who had access to the car and fits within the five-foot-five height range."

Yet another collective gasp swept over the courtroom. Through it, Prosecutor Lang was heard shouting, "Objection: the defence is referring to facts not in evidence. Sarah Brenner is not on trial here."

"Maybe she should be," Tanning shouted back. His words caused the gasping crowd to erupt into a jumpy mob.

Firestone saw what he could only assume was Ms. Brenner; a tall sophisticated blonde wearing dark glasses run out the door as Harmon began to scream for order and the court security officers began sifting through the audience and removing those who were being the most disruptive.

After a few moments, the courtroom was back in order.

"I'm filing a motion for dismissal." Tanning declared. "The prosecution has what I have; they clearly don't have their case in order and are blaming me for it..."

"I object again, your honor. We're passed the point for motions to dismiss. It is up to the jury to decide how the case should resolve." Lang pushed.

"With all due respect to Prosecutor Lang, the jury has to base their decision on the facts that they hear. Prosecutor Lang is not allowing legal evidence that should exonerate my client to be heard in this court, so the jury is going to be unfairly biased against my client." Tanning said.

"Your honor, this *supposed* evidence is not what's in my case file and this would not be the first time Tanning stood accused of fabricating the components of a case to fit his premise..."

Tanning turned to yell at her, but Judge Harmon slammed his gavel relentlessly, not allowing him, or anyone else, to get a word in.

Firestone strained to hear what was said as both sides approached Harmon and everyone lowered their voices. He heard Harmon whisper, "Ms. Lang, you are out of order. You cannot make accusations about anyone in my courtroom without proof. Although Mr. Tanning is also throwing around some serious accusations, at least he has a file for us to review."

Harmon then spoke up for the entire room to hear, "I cannot ignore this potential for new evidence, so we are going to take a two-hour recess. The counsellors will spend the next two hours discussing these matters and I will be available to them in chambers if they need."

"Our first order of business will be to determine whose forensic report is valid and the next step will be to determine whether a deal can be reached. If a deal is reached, I will dismiss the jury and we will negotiate a sentence. If a deal is not reached however, whatever evidence is valid will be presented to the jury and the defendant's fait will be in their hands once again; fair enough?"

Everyone seemed to nod along so Harmon banged his gavel, confirming the order, and everyone dispersed for lunch.

Firestone originally planned to compose the files that Daniel had asked him for when they spoke on the phone earlier. He planned to return to the law firm, hand those files in, and learn the outcome of the Brenner case from whatever sources he could find, but a return call from his construction foreman put his plans on hold.

The foreman ultimately refused to help Firestone in any way and the two men ended up arguing.

The next thing Firestone knew, a security guard was tapping him on the shoulder.

"Sir, I'm sorry but I have to ask you to either quiet down or leave the building because court is resuming..."

Firestone spun around until his eyes found a clock. He realized that he had been arguing with the foreman for the entire two hour recess and he was officially late for meeting Daniel. He wrapped up his argument with the foreman abruptly and recognized that he was in no shape to deal with Daniel, so he returned to a seat at the Brenner trial.

Firestone found a different seat on the prosecution side of the courtroom and when everyone rose to acknowledge Harmon's return to the bench, Firestone happened to look over and see that Tanning seemed different.

Before the break, Tanning had the entire room at his mercy, but now he was soaked in sweat. He was swaying like he was about to faint and he was scratching at his face and hands. *Something was wrong with Tanning.*

By the time Harmon sat down, Tanning collapsed and began convulsing. A panic swept through the courtroom and by the time Firestone cut through the panicked crowd, Tanning was dead.

Chapter 4

The police and medical response to the courthouse was instant. The court officers reprimanded Brenner back into custody and the jury and spectators were evacuated, but the fast police response made certain that they got statements from everyone, including Firestone, before they dispersed.

Firestone prepared to go back to the office and face some heavy music from Daniel, when Judge Harmon stopped him, and called him in to chambers.

Harmon began speaking before the door was even closed behind them. "Tony, it's good to see you; I hear that you're a private investigator now, is that true?"

Firestone sat casually, "Yes, I'm making more in a month than I made in six at the bureau and I married Leah..." Firestone then gave a disarming chuckle.

Harmon gave Firestone a warm smile similar to that of a proud father as they both sat. After an awkward moment of silence, Firestone asked, "Why am I here, Harmon?"

Harmon confidently stated, "Tanning died of an allergic reaction to peanuts. Tanning was murdered."

Firestone was surprised. Tanning's peanut allergy wasn't any secret. Tanning was always incredibly cautious about what he ate because he knew his allergy was severe enough to kill him, but just because some peanut residue managed to escape Tanning's vigilance didn't necessarily mean that he was murdered. At the same time, it was unlike Harmon to jump to conclusions.

Firestone asked, "Are you sure? Tanning hasn't been dead for even four hours yet, so they couldn't have determined how the peanuts got into his system. Maybe the deli made an error and Tanning ate peanuts by mistake…"

Harmon nodded and explained, "They're doing an autopsy, but everyone concerned by his death isn't waiting for the report because we already know that the level of peanut oil in Tanning's system was way too heavy to be accidental; the paramedics said they could smell it on him. The police also found a note in an inside pocket of Tanning's jacket. It read: 'another one down'. Officer Michaels and Prosecutor Lang are convinced it's a serial killing thing. They are already filing charges against Brenner. They think

Brenner's a serial killer that's targeting lawyers. Two lawyers were killed in the accident that Brenner stood accused of perpetrating today; Tanning would therefore be 'another one down.'"

Firestone fidgeted. To him, a note like that could mean anything; it could have been from one of Tanning's associates saying *another case down.* Firestone also felt that Harmon knew he was reaching.

"I take it you disagree with the theory?" Firestone asked.

"Tanning showed me the evidence he had."

"The file he was waving around in court?" Firestone asked for clarity.

"Right," Harmon confirmed, "Tanning felt that it cleared Brenner and he showed it to me because he was convinced that the police and prosecution were stacking the decks against Brenner; he didn't trust them to make an appropriate deal. I have to admit, he had me convinced."

"Convince me..." An intrigued Firestone purred.

"Tanning had a forensics report with all of the correct watermarks and stamping. It verified that the driver's seat of the car in question was too far forward for a man of Brenner's size to have been driving it when it was submerged in the pond..." Harmon paused dramatically, as if his statement was a revelation, but it wasn't.

After a respectful moment, Firestone delicately pushed things along by saying, "Yeah, Tanning said that in court..."

"Yes, but Tanning's report *proved* it. Pond scum lodged in the seat adjustment rig verified the positioning of the rig. According to the report, the scum couldn't have dried the way it did if the rig was adjusted after submerging in the pond, so there is no way the rigs positioning could have been the result of a forensic mistake..."

"Its illogical to assume that Tanning drove that car into those lawyers, got out, and let someone else adjust the seat, drive it as far as it could go in its damaged state, and dump it..."

Firestone had to admit that the driver's seat position was damning enough evidence that a lawyer with the showmanship that Tanning had could sway a jury with it, but it was not necessarily Brenner's saving grace.

Firestone argued, "Brenner could have squished himself in uncomfortably to commit the crime. According to the testimony I heard today, Brenner was too drunk to feel much and he was plenty smart enough to make an attempt to make himself appear innocent."

"I agree," Harmon asserted, "But I still have several problems with the case against Brenner. First, the investigating officers should have worked harder to verify that no one except Brenner could have been driving that night and they didn't; that's the definition of reasonable doubt..."

"Second, Tanning's report also showed evidence of a text on Brenner's phone from an as-yet unidentified number. The person behind the mystery text asked Brenner to meet them in that park by the pond that night."

"The prosecution's case suggests that being in the park that night was Landon Brenner's idea; him being invited to go there destroys that entire concept..."

"According to Tanning, Brenner's drinking schedule was predictable. Tanning's theory was that someone waited for Brenner to become mindlessly drunk before they set up a meeting with him at the park via text. Drunk, Brenner went to the park while that someone else killed those lawyers using his car. They then ditched Brenner's car in the pond and left Brenner there for the police to find. Frankly, I think Tanning's theory ties up more loose ends than the prosecution's case does..."

"Sounds like a solid theory," Firestone admitted.

Harmon nodded enthusiastically and went on, "Third, Brenner supposedly battered his wife and caused a car accident, but he was only soaked in pond water; there wasn't a single scratch or bruise on him; that's impossible, right?"

Firestone had to admit that committing both a brutal beating and a car accident are difficult to do without getting hurt yourself, but Firestone had seen killers do it in the past. Wearing gloves and a mask are easy ways to minimize scrapes. Still, it was clear Tanning had brought forward a strong case for Brenner's potential innocence.

"Why don't you dismiss the case?" Firestone questioned.

"The chief defence attorney died under suspicious circumstances, so, of course, I'm declaring a mistrial, but, like I said already, Prosecutor Lang intends to re-file and add additional charges related to Tanning's death against Brenner."

"That's her right..."

"But Firestone, I've already seen Lang's existing case against Brenner and her files do not match Tanning's. She believes she has reason to re-file based on what she has, but I don't know if I can agree with her in good conscious."

Firestone leaned in as his intrigue began to consume him. Harmon explained, "Her reports show no evidence of an abnormal seat position, a text to Brenner, or anything else that Tanning seemed to have." Harmon paused and rubbed his nose, like he was choosing his words carefully, before saying, "Either Tanning did fabricate his evidence, Lang lied, or the police lied to Lang; two out of those three possibilities imply that someone within our legal force is taking steps to *ensure* Brenner goes down. Firestone, we're men of the law and we have a responsibility to get to the truth."

Firestone began sense what Harmon was about to ask. He wanted to say *something or anything* to stop him, but because he didn't know what to say, he simply listened uncomfortably as Harmon gently asked for the impossible, "The police can't be trusted to investigate this matter objectively and I cannot legally investigate it, but you can."

"I've reached out to some friends on the police force and they are assigning a detective from the Internal Affairs division to partner with you. Your job is to find out whether or not Brenner is actually innocent of the vehicular homicides he stood accused of today as well as Tanning's death. If he is innocent, you must apprehend the real killer and expose any corruption in the system you come across."

"The city has also agreed to pay your fees as a private investigator, but you must keep this investigation as secret as possible. We expect you to maintain your job at the law firm and you cannot tell Leah, or anyone else who is not directly involved in the investigation, what you're up to..."

It was now Firestone's turn to carefully choose his words. After a moment of consideration, he said, "I don't think I'm your man. I've never cared for Internal Affairs and I can't keep secrets from my wife..."

Judge Harmon interrupted, "I understand how you feel, but you'll be investigating the local police and not your former co-workers at the FBI; doesn't that make it better?"

Firestone shook his head, "Cops are cops, regardless of rank, office, or jurisdiction and who I investigate doesn't change the fact that you're asking me to keep secrets and alienate..."

Harmon interrupted again; this time, he spoke more condescendingly. "It is also entirely possible that Tanning and Brenner have suckered me into their show and Brenner is actually a serial killer who betrayed Tanning a little too quickly..."

"Firestone, if more lawyers get killed because we failed to convict Brenner when we could have, two terrible things will happen. One, those hypothetical lawyers will lose their lives and, two, upon their deaths, those lawyers' cases will be reviewed which means that criminals of all shapes and sizes could escape justice on technicalities."

"This city is still recovering after the terrorist attacks that you resolved and those criminals could then go on to steal, sicken, and kill people who absolutely don't need more strife in their lives."

"Firestone, police are unfairly criticized enough already. You can give them a fair shake. Also, if this investigation comes out of the shadows too much, well, we don't need that either, do we? I need you on this Firestone and I need your discretion. "

Actually, Firestone felt that Harmon was being overdramatic, but he couldn't deny that the man had a point, so he asked, "Can I speak with Brenner before I commit to anything?"

Harmon was surprised, "Yes; Brenner is still in the contempt hold here at the courthouse; you can speak with him there, but would he really sway you one way or the other?"

"Yes, if I have to come to the man's defence, I need to know if there's something worth defending..."

The next thing Firestone knew, he was standing face-to-face with Landon Brenner, talking to him through cell bars.

Chapter 5

Harmon dramatically said, "Mr. Brenner, this is Special Investigator Anthony Firestone. He's giving your case a second look. Answer his questions like your freedom depends on him because it just might..." Harmon then left, leaving the two men alone to speak privately.

Firestone evaluated Brenner in silence for several moments. Even though Firestone knew almost nothing about Brenner, or Family Page, or the crimes Brenner allegedly committed; his assessment told him that Brenner was **not** a murderous man.

Firestone noted that Brenner seemed anxious and tearful. He seemed to be grieving for Tanning and he was obviously concerned about what Tanning's death meant for his future. Brenner was also a stick of a man; he was tall and slender and lacked the grizzle of a man that beat his ex-wife to near-death or force peanut oil down Tanning's throat.

Brenner finally broke the silence, saying, "Firestone; where have I heard that name before? Aren't you some kind of anti-terrorism specialist?"

"I was an FBI Agent; I'm retired from that now..." After answering Brenner, Firestone returned to silent revelry.

Brenner grew impatient quickly, "The judge said that you had questions for me..."

"I do..." Firestone could see Brenner's temper building, so he baited Brenner with more silence. Firestone felt that he needed to gage what Brenner would do.

It took less than ten seconds for Brenner to take that bait. He outstretched his arms in an impatient gesture before demanding, "So start asking damn it..."

He had a strong temper. Firestone supposed that Brenner may have caused that deadly car accident and assaulted his wife in a fit of temperamental rage, but fits of rage tend not to allow for preplanning. Firestone failed to see how Brenner could have avoided scrapes and bruises without preplanning and protective gear. *Harmon was right; this read more like an elaborate frame than an open and shut murder case.*

"What happened the night of the car wreck, Brenner?"

As fast as Brenner's temper appeared, it died and he became resigned, "I don't know. I drank a lot that day. Daily called me in to his office to tell me he was quitting. I smashed a few windows and vases and I cut up some paintings and keyed some cars at Sarah's the week before..." Brenner spoke like smashing his ex-wife's belongings was the most natural thing in the world.

"Sarah wanted me charged; Daily wanted no part of that."

"Daily and I argued and I roughed him up a bit, but once the security pulled me off of him, Sarah consumed my thoughts. All I could think about was undoing our divorce. I drank some, called her, drank some more while we talked, and drank even more once I got to her place..."

"Did you beat your wife?"

"We slapped each other around from time to time, but I *never* hurt her the way Tanning said she said I did and like I said, I was wasted that night, but I *know* that night I loved her..."

Brenner was no candidate for sainthood, but his tone, his words, and his every expression appeared too genuine to be faked.

Firestone now firmly believed that Tanning and Harmon were right to believe in Brenner. Firestone switched his questioning from evaluating Brenner's character to determining who would frame him.

"You said you drank at Sarah's. Did she invite you there or did you invite yourself?"

"A bit of both: initially, she wanted nothing to with me, but I kept pushing and when I showed up and explained how done I was with Daily, I wore her down."

Firestone thought it was interesting that Sarah Brenner was intrigued *only after* problems between Daily and her husband became known.

"So you drank with Sarah all night?"

"She took my keys for liquor runs several times..." *So she had the car.* Amazingly, Brenner didn't seem to be doing the same math as everyone defending him was. Brenner didn't seem to have any suspicions of his wife, but obviously, Tanning knew the significance of what Brenner had just relayed and that was why Tanning was so accusatory of Sarah in court.

"How did you get to the park where you were arrested?" Firestone pressured.

Brenner shrugged, "I was all but blacked out by then. I could've even been carried to that bench by elves for all I know. I woke up about two days later in lock up. I do remember freaking out while I watched my car sink; you know, like you remember a dream..."

"How did you feel about Tanning?"

"He was a good listener and a badass lawyer. He promised to take Daily's place pro-bono after he saved me from jail. I can't believe that a stupid mistake at a deli could ruin my life..."

Firestone was taken aback, "You knew Tanning died from his peanut allergy?"

"I assumed so; he stopped eating about halfway through his meal because he suspected he was reacting to it..."

That statement raised another question. *If Tanning knew he was having a reaction, why didn't he medicate himself for it?* The simple answer was that someone stopped him.

"Mr. Brenner, did Tanning take anything for his allergy suspicion?" Firestone interrogated.

"No, some blonde was brought in choking. Everybody knew Tanning had epinephrine on him so they came to him for help. She walked off with everything he had before we even started eating."

Firestone was satisfied that he now had a jumping-off point for his investigation so he said, "Thank-you, Mr. Brenner..." and started walking away.

Brenner called after him, "Are you going to help me?"

"Yes, Mr. Brenner, I'm going to try..."

Harmon was waiting outside the door and heard Firestone's last line to Brenner. The two talked while they walked back and settled into Harmon's chambers.

"So you're in?"

Firestone reluctantly surrendered, "I'm in; is there a timeline here?"

"Lang will want Brenner behind bars before the new DA is elected; that gives you three months..."

Firestone cringed. He was about to argue that three months wasn't enough time to solve such a complex case, especially while potentially bucking police corruption, but before Firestone could continue negotiating, a knock came at the door. Both men stood, but Harmon answered the door. Harmon then stepped aside to give the woman at the door a clear path to Firestone.

Harmon said, "Special Detective Firestone, meet your new partner: IA Investigator: Amanda Toller."

Firestone immediately recognized Toller; he had mistakenly assumed that she was Sarah Brenner when he saw slip away during the courthouse chaos that Tanning had prompted.

Toller was tall, blonde, and slender. She was dressed as a high-fashion business woman with a pink button-up blouse, black fitted skirt, and expensive high-heeled shoes. Her hair was done up tight and she had narrow features, good makeup, and a hard expression.

All of a sudden, that reliable feeling in the pit of his stomach reappeared; that feeling in his gut told Firestone that Scarleto was guilty back in the

Carlton Tower firestorm and now it was telling him that the next guilty party was before him.

A blonde woman, who perhaps needed epinephrine, and who was connected to Tanning from being in the courtroom...

Firestone's gut told him she was Tanning's killer, but was he right and was she Brenner's framer too? He'd have to work very hard to get those answers.

All she said was, "Are you ready to start?"

PART TWO – NEW PARTNER, OLD PROBLEMS

Chapter 6

Firestone gently convinced Toller that their investigation should pick up in the morning, but he regretted taking that break almost instantly. Firestone was disappointed to return to a lonely hotel room. Firestone presumed that Leah had awoken and went to work as his note instructed, but she failed to return that night. Given the choice, he would rather have spent his time investigating rather than sleeping alone.

Firestone had to admit to himself that night wouldn't be the first time Leah had slept in her office, but Firestone had hoped he could explain himself to Leah. He got caught up investigating and failed to submit the files he promised her and Daniel; that couldn't have gone over well. He also had that second fight with their construction foreman during the trial intermission and now their renovation was in limbo; he felt that was a conversation they should have face to face.

Firestone felt that he and Leah needed to work on their communication and him failing to deliver at work in combination with her failing to come home at night wasn't helping solve their communication issues.

The next morning, Firestone wanted to go to his office and talk to Leah and Daniel there, but because he had made her wait already, Toller was unwilling to postpone their investigation any longer. She dragged him to police headquarters before he could say anything. Once there, they rode the elevator down to the cities' chief forensics lab in the basement.

The basement lab did not look like a basement because of its bright pale blue walls, glass doors, and unique black floors. Everyone was dressed in sparkling white lab coats, doctor's masks, and lab goggles.

They walked past the various testing labs to a room marked: *Report Storage.*

The Report Storage area was a maze of stacks of standard three-drawer metallic filing cabinets all marked in code. It was also a lot darker and daunting than the rest of the lab seemed. It was there that Firestone found himself face-to-face with another familiar face: Forensic Scientist, Dawson Sour.

Years ago, when Firestone was an FBI Agent investigating the Carlton Tower terror attack, Sour was essential to solving the attack and the surrounding conspiracy that led to a second strike.

Firestone recognized that Sour's science ultimately saved many lives and Firestone's career because Firestone put a lot on the line to stop Scarleto and regularly lost sight of evidence, procedure, and stopping the men around Scarleto, but Sour redeemed him by keeping those details in mind and ultimately building a case that the courts could cling to.

Sour had also become a personal friend and attended the Firestone's wedding.

Back then, Sour was a lanky boy with wild red hair. Over the years, Sour had bulked up, shaved his hair down, and traded in his overwhelmingly boyish love of science for *some* professionalism.

Sour was filing some folders away but greeted them kindly when they walked in. "Anthony Firestone, how are you man? How's the wife?" He questioned with an enthusiastic handshake.

"We're both wonderful…" Firestone lied because now wasn't the time to discuss his and Leah's struggles.

Toller interjected, "We're reviewing allegations made by late defence attorney Fred Tanning. We need to speak to this lab's supervisor."

"You've got him; well, I'm the supervisor of this shift anyway." Sour turned back Firestone and spoke with a smile, "I was promoted largely because of your recommendation, but unfortunately, the promotion is temporary. I'm only a supervisor for a few more days while the regular supervisor is out assisting with an archeological dig…"

Firestone laughed, "You earned my recommendation and at least you're in line to advance…"

Sour nodded happily and Firestone would have liked to keep the mood more noncontroversial, but he could tell by Toller's facial and body language that keeping things light was fast becoming not an option. He dove into their investigation before Toller could bring out her claws. "We heard that some of the forensics done on Landon Brenner's car points to another driver…"

"Yes, Prosecutor Lang apparently sent someone over to double-check the reports last night, but they should be done now and People versus Landon Brenner should be filed right here..." Sour opened a filing cabinet behind him and began fingering his way through the files inside.

After a few seconds he paused and then started over. After his second lap through the drawer he began mumbling under his breath and it became clear that he wasn't finding what he needed. He began pulling files from the drawer and leafing through them, likely checking if the papers he needed were misfiled.

"Is there a problem?" Toller growled.

Sour continued leafing for a moment before he re-packed the drawer. He closed it and, empty-handed, explained, "The collection of our lab reports for that case doesn't seem to be here, but it's not a problem. Paperwork gets moved around a lot, especially when the case is moving through the courts, so we keep copies in the cabinet in the supervisor office for occasions such as these. Please follow me."

He led them out of the records area and into a posh glass office across the hallway. Firestone and

Toller settled into seats while Sour leafed through yet another cabinet. After a moment, Sour settled into his desk, reading the file as he sat, but they could tell from his expression that something was still wrong.

"Well, this is your file. It is stamped as having had a copy of it sent to Fred Tanning's office, but..."

Sour got lost in the file and failed to finish the sentence, so Firestone asked, "But what?"

Sour looked up, "Tiffany Smith is another supervisor here. She normally looks after one of the nightshifts, but she's recently had some pregnancy complications and has been off on sick leave for the last six months; all of the supervisor's have been circulating through taking care of her shift. I know for a fact that she was not working on these dates and yet she's listed as the supervisor responsible for the case."

"We'll need to speak with this Tiffany Smith..." Toller grumbled as she speedily scribbled notes in a worn notepad.

"And whatever supervisor *was* working those dates..." Firestone added.

"Sure, I don't know who that would have been because I was vacationing in Paris that week, but I can get that information for you easily enough."

Sour then turned his attention back to the file briefly before saying. "That's not the only thing sending up flags for me here though. According to this, all of the forensics points to your guy: Landon Brenner. There's nothing here that points to someone else, like you said there would be..."

Firestone believed that Sour could be missing such a small detail, so he clarified, "Our source mentioned that the driver's seat position pointed to someone smaller than Brenner being the driver."

Sour skimmed over the file again with that in mind, but he ultimately said, "Not according to this; see?" Sour tried to hand Firestone the file so he could read through it for himself, but before he could take it, Toller snatched it away and started reading it.

While Toller studied the paper, Firestone started asking some important questions, "Is Tiffany Smith a good employee?"

"Well, we're on opposite shifts, so I didn't know her very well personally, but we regularly briefed each other as we passed the proverbial baton between our shifts. She seemed very nice. She was eager to answer questions and offer help. Everything she did was mistake-free and when she fell ill, the entire lab put together gift baskets and cards for her. I can't think of anyone who disliked her."

Firestone bit his lip as he asked, "Sour, did you have anything to do with this case whatsoever?"

"No, like I said, I was in France while this case was in processing and the car was impounded after midnight, so it would have been handled by the nightshift staff and not my shift. Why?"

Firestone remembered that he was supposed to leave as many people as possible in the dark about the entire mystery, but Firestone saw Sour's potential to help the case more-so than corrupt it so he hesitantly explained, "Dawson, I've got be honest; we're here because Fred Tanning was murdered. He apparently had some reports that contradicted yours, but his copy of this case appears to be stolen off his body."

"My God..." Sour whispered.

Firestone nodded and continued, "Now we need to determine how bad the damage is. We need to determine if what's on paper here," He gestured to the file in Toller's hand, "Is really what was found at the crime scene. If not, the obvious conclusion we draw is that someone with department access is going to great lengths to obscure the truth of what really happened in the Brenner case, including killing Tanning."

"Of course;" Sour said, "Just tell me what you need and you'll have it."

"In addition to the contact information of the two supervisors that we've already asked for, I need the names of everyone with access to the forensic files..."

Sour seemed to lose some of his helpful enthusiasm as he explained, "That's a long list. All of our files need to be accessed by a lot of different people 24 hours a day. You saw the records area, nothing's locked or guarded, but we do have surveillance cameras and I should be able to backtrack through the computer systems' history and find out who published the version of the file that I have here; that should tell you who was responsible..."

"Good; do that."

Toller jumped in, "Firestone, can I talk to you outside?"

They stepped outside, leaving Sour to dig out some information. "I don't like this," Toller quietly hissed, "Do you realize that your buddy there is in perhaps the best position to build this cover-up and you not only tipped him off that we're on to him, but also, you are giving him the reins he needs to frame someone else. In investigations like this one, you cannot trust anyone. You need to stop taking people at their word."

"Fair enough, but you need to warm up a little." Firestone instructed, "Not everyone we'll come across is going to be dirty and we need experts like Sour on our side..."

Toller moved like she was going to spit more anger at him, but Firestone's cell phone interrupted her. The name and number on the screen told him that it was his wife, Leah, calling from her office back at the law firm.

"This is my wife at my other job; I need to answer it."

"Fine."

Firestone didn't like pausing Toller on such a bitter note, so he let the phone ring a little longer while he offered, "I have another friend, like me, she's retired from law enforcement, so she doesn't know anything about any of this. She's brilliant with computers and can easily double-check what Sour gives us. If she fines flaws, I'll be the first to admit that I'm wrong and we'll take Sour in..."

Firestone's phone stopped ringing. He cringed because he knew that he'd missed his call from Leah.

"I like that idea," Toller purred, "But I'm not interested in getting you into a deeper conflict of interest, so I'm getting my own computer expert..."

"You do that; I have to talk to my wife..."

Toller and Firestone finally went their separate ways, but neither of them told the other the whole truth about what they do next.

Chapter 7

Firestone's first stop was to see Leah. He found her in her office. As he walked up, he noted that she was drawn to tears and talking on her office phone.

Although she down-played her accessories and makeup, today what little there was make-up was quite noticeably streaming down her face.

Prior to marrying him and starting her career at the law firm, Leah had been Firestone's partner for 11 years. She helped him takedown Scarleto and Chang *and* she survived months of torture to do so. It took a lot to get her that shaken up, so Firestone was worried.

As soon as she saw him through the glass of her office walls and door; she hung up suddenly, scrubbed the tears and streams of makeup from her face with a tissue, and ran up to greet him. She kissed him on the cheek and wrapped him in a tender hug.

Firestone chuckled nervously. He was fearful about being bothersome to her, but he wanted to address his concerns about her, so he asked, "Leah, who was that on the phone?"

Leah seemed to panic. She pushed herself away from him suddenly, "What's this about the phone?"

"You were on the phone just now and you're crying. Who was it? What did they say? You know you can talk to me about anything, right?"

She started to sob. "Anthony, I thought I lost you. I heard there was a death at the courthouse and I knew that's where you went and then you didn't answer when I called..."

He considered explaining that he slept at their hotel the previous night and had she come home for a proper sleep, seeing him there would have cancelled her worries, but instead he laughingly said, "Oh, Leah, I'm sorry. I got distracted helping the police with their investigation into *Fred Tanning's* death. I was a witness, after all, and I missed your call. I tried to call you back but I couldn't track you down..."

Leah took a long moment to straighten up. About four more tissues were sacrificed to the cause, but eventually she whispered, "Ok, everything's fine now..."

"Where were you last night, Lee? You had me worried and there's thing's we need to discuss, not the least of which is our house…"

She pressed her palms on his chest, playfully slowing him down, "One thing at a time: last night, I had to work late because I'd missed the morning. I don't care about the house anymore; pay more, pay less, or hire someone else, or sell it; I don't care; I just want that off my to-do list… and as for whatever else you want to talk about: both of us have to wait because I have even more work that needs to take precedence and you have other things that need your attention more also."

Firestone wasn't convinced. There was a twinge in Leah's voice that confirmed there was more she wanted to say. He suspected that she was lying about where she was and he suspected that the words they weren't saying needed to be tended to more than their work did, but unfortunately, the office wasn't the place to get into an argument.

He simply asked, "Are you sure?" He made sure to let the tone of his voice, his eyes, and his touch *show* her how intensely he cared and how willing he was to help her.

Leah only nodded unconvincingly.

Firestone intended to pry more, but Leah said, "Daniel needs to see you about some outstanding paperwork."

Firestone suddenly remembered that he didn't have the files Daniel wanted and he failed to deliver them after he promised he would yesterday.

Firestone got the feeling that if he wanted to keep working with Daniel, cuddling Leah would have to wait. He reluctantly said, "Ok, I better go see him then, but how about dinner or movie tonight? We have a dust-free kitchen available and there will be no hammer noise to interrupt us..."

Leah suddenly became disorientated again. She said, "Oh, I have something I need to do tonight; maybe tomorrow?"

Firestone was not satisfied, but he wanted to be Leah's safe place to land and not another addition to her stress, so he respectfully nodded and reluctantly dragged his feet across the hallway to speak with Daniel.

Daniel Fong was 64 years old, but he had the energy of most men half his age. He had a long white beard, long white mustache, and beautifully trimmed white hair.

Daniel always wore the sharpest suits. Today's suit had a navy blue jacket and pants with a slightly lighter blue shirt, a bright neon blue tie, a pocket handkerchief that matched the tie, and dark brown belt that coordinated with dark brown shoes.

Seeing that Daniel was alone in the office and not on the phone, Firestone let himself in. To alert Daniel to his being there, he said, "Knock-Knock."

Daniel was surprisingly warm and bubbly, "Hi Tony have a seat."

Daniel was a difficult man to read. He rarely showed emotion with his face or voice, but Firestone expected him to be noticeably angrier than he was because Daniel always expected things to be done when he asked for them and he expected things to be done to the highest quality; Firestone failed on both counts lately.

Daniel's office was unique and colourful. The entire law firm had the same papery golden walls with artistic wooden features that transported a person to Asia, but, unlike Leah's virtually empty office, with a simple desk and basic comfortable guest chairs, some photos, and a flowering plant in the corner; Daniel had a desk that was a converted airplane wing and ornate antique cast-iron guest chairs that were quite uncomfortable.

Firestone sat but squirmed in his uncomfortable seat while Daniel explained, "Someone from the courthouse came by yesterday and dropped off a judicial order that informs us that you'll be splitting your time between us and a private criminal investigation assignment for Judge Harmon..."

Daniel's tone was clearly asking Firestone to elaborate, but Firestone knew he could not indulge him, so Firestone responded simply. "Yeah, it shouldn't be a problem though. I'm expected to keep working here, so once we're done here, I'm going to be meeting with Angelique. I'll get the last of the reports and photos we need for the Sullivan, Donahue, and Smith files. I'm afraid I don't have them yet; I'm sorry..."

Daniel casually waved off Firestone's confession of failure and said, "Sounds perfect; I'll be advising the rest of the firm to only use your services when absolutely necessary, to give you more freedom for the duration of your special assignment as well..."

"Much appreciated..." Leah was consuming Firestone's mind. Finally, he said, "Daniel, we need to talk about your sister..."

"Whatever do you mean?" Firestone's comment clearly surprised Daniel.

"Leah seems tearful, tired, and shaken lately. I know that something is wrong, but she won't talk to me about it. I've tried prying and I've tried being patient, but the only thing that's changing is that she is becoming more distant..."

Daniel's expressionless face was suddenly muddied with a mix of emotions. Firestone suddenly suspected that Leah was confiding in her big brother, but Daniel gave him nothing, only saying, "I suppose that Leah has seemed a little preoccupied lately, but I thought she was seeing a therapist already to help her cope with her torture, her injuries, and the loss of her FBI career..."

"She was... she still is, as far as I know, but it's obviously not enough."

Daniel cleared his throat uncomfortably and whispered, "Then I'll talk to her...soon."

Firestone stood, pulled Daniel into a serious handshake, and stared him down to ensure his sincerity got through as he said, "Thank-you, I'll give her whatever she needs."

Daniel pulled away. As though Firestone had somehow backed him into a corner, Daniel's demeanor reverted back to that of the tyrannical boss Firestone knew so well.

"Perhaps now, you need to get back to work." Daniel stoically warned, "I needed those files from you yesterday, now I won't be able to meet with two of those clients for another two weeks. They are unhappy and I am unimpressed but... I'm trying to understand, given everything you have going on."

"I respect you, Anthony; you treat my sister very well and consistently do good work, despite all of the distractions. I also understand that this judicial order comes from a higher office than mine, so your new assignment will need to take priority over your responsibilities here, but I still need what I need..."

Firestone nodded and the two men parted on good terms, but there was something about Daniel's tone that suggested to Firestone that they weren't just talking about paperwork. *Again, Firestone longed for a simple yet thorough explanation of what the people around him were thinking and feeling, but he knew that he needed to scratch and claw for every clue.*

Firestone felt very frustrated as he travelled to his next stop; Angelique Marceau's home.

Angelique was born in the Caribbean. She lived there until she married her husband and they followed his career to Washington.

Angelique had beautiful dark skin, crazy-curly black hair, and a seductively French accent. She was about 300 pounds over a healthy weight, but she dressed nicely for her shape.

She liked colourfully patterned blouses, fitted skirts, and fashionable heels. She wore a lot of jewellery and streaked her hair colorfully. She changed the color of her hair streaks regularly; today, they were gold.

Angelique was Firestone and Leah's mutual best friend and she was a computer expert since pocket calculators were still just a concept in someone's head. She used to be the FBI's foremost Cyber Analyst and IT Superwoman, but she retired from the FBI very shortly after Firestone and Leah married. She now did private pay-as-you-go IT work for some small businesses, neighbours, and friends.

"Anthony, how are you handsome?" She asked as he let himself into her garage office where she was already working.

The garage was built to hold two cars. The Marceau's shiny black sedan took up half the space and all of the regular home and garden tools were clustered on the same side as the car to allow Angelique's half of the garage to be professional, spacious, and comfortable; which it was.

The walls were lime-washed exposed brick and the decor was Angelique's unique blend of family photos, unique storage solutions, and technology wires.

"Fine, just fine, and you?" Firestone huffed unconvincingly.

She pulled him in for a hug, "All is good with us, although I suspect all is not so good with you; is Leah alright?"

"She seems to be struggling, as a matter of fact; I talked to Daniel about it, but I think a call from you would help a lot..."

"Of course, I've been meaning to treat her to coffee. We have a lot to discuss... mainly you..." She said with a laugh.

Firestone chuckled in embarrassment. Although she was a happily married woman, for as long as they had known each other, Angelique made a joke out of pretending to have a crush on Firestone.

With their regular playful banter over with, Angelique handed him a stack of files and explained, "Here are those files you asked me for from the law firm."

Firestone finally had Daniel's files.

Firestone took the files and added, "I'm working on something else. It's a separate project for Judge Harmon: very covert."

"Ok..."

"I need anything and everything you can give me on the murder case against Landon Brenner. I'm giving it a second look. I also need a full workup on Fred Tanning, Brenner's lawyer, specifically I need to know if there was anyone in both of their lives mad enough to sabotage Brenner by killing Tanning..."

Angelique's ear perked, "What's going on, Tony?"

"Fred Tanning was killed and the working theory is that someone killed Tanning as part of an elaborate cover-up against Tanning's latest client: Brenner. The cover-up extends into the CSI Lab. I need to explore every avenue and every person."

"Like the good old days..." She said as she dove into her search with a playful eye-roll.

Firestone nodded and added, "One slight complication; Sour is a supervisor at the CSI lab. He said he was vacationing in France while the suspicious activity happened; I need you to check on that..."

She turned back towards him, "You don't think he's involved..."

Her concern was clear to him, so Firestone shaped his words into a playful whisper, "No, but as my new partner eagerly pointed out, we have a responsibllity to suspect everyone at this point in the investigation..."

Angelique laughed and shifted her focus back to what Firestone was looking for. As she typed, she questioned him further, "It sounds to me like you don't like your new partner..."

Firestone stepped closer to her and began massaging her shoulders as he explained, "She's a real ice princess and honestly, I want you to look into her too. Her name's Amanda Toller and she's from Internal Affairs."

Firestone then turned away from Angelique in a state of confliction, "I don't know what it is about her; maybe it's because she's not Leah and she's not *likable*, but something about her just turns my stomach."

Firestone kept spinning on his heels, "I don't know if it's her or if I just don't feel the same passion for this case that I did as an FBI Agent. I mean, I've got another job that doesn't stop because I'm investigating this cold case-turned-conspiracy, Leah needs me, and…"

When his words faded, Angelique stared back at him and squeezed one of his hands in a wordless but effective show of support because although Firestone was fragmented, Angelique understood his sentiment.

Angelique had assisted Firestone on enough investigations to recognize that what made him great was his ability to get into the minds of both his victim and his killer.

When he thought like his victim, he uncovered what people in their life deserved sympathy and which ones deserved suspicion; that line of thinking helped him determine who the killer was every time. He also figured out why the victim was at their murder scene which told him how the killer did it; but it was Firestone's ability to understand killers that really made him a brilliant agent.

His ability to anticipate his killer's motives and moves meant that he could capture them and convict them by selling jurors the whole story; convictions really needed a *why* and Firestone's investigative mind always delivered that, but Angelique understood that, with his mind already filled with concerns about Leah, concerns about work, and conflicts with the people he was working with, he could not fill his mind with somebody else's thoughts.

They both felt that Firestone needed to talk more, but his phone interrupted them. "Speaking of the ice princess, I think this is her..." he said as he read the ID on the screen. He didn't recognize the number, but a name would have been tied to the number if it was a professional organization or someone he'd added to his contact list, so, by process of elimination, it had to be Toller.

Angelique nodded and turned back to her screen, giving him the indication of privacy he needed in order to take the call.

Firestone barely squeaked out a greeting before he was forced into a moment of listening. After that moment, Firestone headed back to his car, almost in a panic. As he walked, Angelique heard him say, "I don't understand how they could throw you out, but I'll be right there..."

Suddenly, a tracking program that Angelique forgot she was running consumed her screen. She studied it for a second before realizing what it meant. Upon reaching that critical realization, she started running after Anthony and calling for him, but she was too late. His car was already too far gone for him to see or hear her trying to flag her down.

She jogged back to her 'office' and began frantically dialing Firestone's number. As she listened to the ringing, anxiously waiting for him to pick up, she whispered, *"C'mon Anthony, answer me. You may be headed for a trap."*

Chapter 8

While Firestone had his chats with Leah, Daniel, and Angelique; Internal Affairs Investigator Amanda Toller, a.k.a the ice princess, was on her own mission. Her first stop was at Carlotta's Coffee Bar to meet with Sarah Brenner.

With a name like Carlotta's, people expected a cafe with a Latin influence. A lot of potential customers turned right back around and took their business elsewhere when they saw baby-blue walls, grey-veined white marble hexagonal tile floors, and white and aluminum furnishings that were as light as air.

Faint classical music wafted through the coffee bar that offered freshly-baked pastries and evening cocktails in addition coffee. While most potential customers refused to take seats, a highly-fashionable Sarah Brenner and Amanda Toller seemed right at home there.

The women greeted one another with smiles and hugs before sitting down to coffees and small jelly-filled pastries. Both women put their black boxy phones on the tabletop as they ate, drank, and spoke.

"How did we end up here, Sarah?" Toller remorsefully whispered. "I planned to be a lawyer right now. I planned to be in a study relationship; perhaps even someone's mother right now, but instead, I'm still a cop and I need to investigate you for murder..."

Sarah Brenner gave Toller a bitter look and then asked, "How long have been friends, Amanda?"

"Since the sixth grade," Toller mumbled.

"Yes; we've trusted each other with our darkest secrets since we were 12, so why are you struggling so hard to stand by the deal that we made? It seems rather simple, I don't report your murdering one of my patients and you cover me while I frame my billionaire husband for his lawyer's murder. We then split my busted husband's fortune evenly a year from now."

Toller eyes bulged and her cheeks immediately reddened. She was shocked that Sarah Brenner had the boldness and dimwittedness necessary to outline their entire plot in such a nonchalant manner and open forum.

She checked the room to make certain they hadn't caught anyone's attention, but in true

Carlotta's fashion, what customers there were in the room were absorbed in their headphones and the free Wi-Fi. *They had gotten lucky.*

Toller quietly and angrily explained, "It *was* a simple agreement when I could utilize Officer Michaels and a few other officers that my position at Internal Affairs gave me power over to lead the case in my preferred direction, however, things have gotten more complicated since the trial began."

Sarah Brenner rolled her eyes, "Is this another argument to get your share of the fortune sooner? I told you on the phone when the police came to my house the night of the accident that a year from now is the best time to transfer the funds..."

Toller got angrier, "My apprehension is not about the money; it's that, what Tanning said was damning and it caught Judge Harmon's attention which took it out of Michaels' hands and has placed it on Anthony Firestone's lap. Do you remember Anthony; the Federal Super-cop that unravelled those serious organized crime conspiracies about a decade ago? The man's an expert..."

Brenner put her hand up, stopping Toller in mid-sentence so that she could point out, "The key words I took from what you just said were *a decade ago.* The man's old news, rusty, slow... I have faith that you can handle him."

"Well, I don't; especially since Tiffany Smith's name has already come up..."

"Tiffany Smith is yours' and Teddy's problem, not mine..." Sarah Brenner spat between sips of coffee.

Toller became so enraged that she began to rise up and out of her seat. "I'm shocked that I have to remind you that you know what's going on with Tiffany. You are in a good position to save her and if you fail to, you're just as responsible as I am under the law."

As the realization of how close potential prison time was actually coming finally set in, the bitter Sarah Brenner suddenly seemed to re-adopt the distressed damsel act that had protected her freedom for this long. "What are we going to do?"

"I have a few more aces to play against Firestone, but you need to start running..."

Both women stood suddenly and grabbed their phones so awkwardly that they didn't realize that they grabbed each other's phones instead of their own.

At the last minute, Sarah Brenner asked, "Where are you going?"

"I need to talk to Teddy and then I need to do some printing at the library. If these things go as I plan, by midnight tonight, one of Firestone's friends will be in jail and Tiffany Smith will be off Firestone's radar. Now run."

Because Toller was cautious about creating an obvious connection between her and Teddy Smith, she never entered his name into her contact list. If she had, she would have sifted through the contact list to try and find his name and she would have realized that she and Sarah Brenner switched phones before that fact doomed her.

She dialed up Teddy Smith. When he answered, she quickly explained, "Baby, I'm sorry but our lucky love boat is sinking quickly. I need to make some calls and pull some paperwork together first, but then I'm coming to your house and I'm bringing my new partner over. He's going to be questioning how deeply Tiffany is involved in the Brenner debacle. He needs to talk to Tiffany, he needs to question her credibility, and he can't suspect *anything*; meaning, I need you to not only convince him that we've never met but also that you despise me..."

"Consider it done," Teddy responded.

Toller then moved unbelievably fast. She traded in Carlotta's for the local library, printed and deleted some vital documents off of her laptop, made copies for Firestone, and then rushed to the Smith house.

It wasn't difficult for a woman so cold tempered as Toller to push way too hard while questioning Tiffany Smith. True to his word, Tiffany's not-so-loving husband, Teddy, did an excellent job of pretending to protect Tiffany. He acted so alienated that he actually locked Toller outside, giving Toller the much-needed opportunity to call Firestone.

Unannounced to both Firestone and Toller, Firestone had interrupted Angelique in the midst of creating a computer program for a security company. Angelique's program matched phone numbers currently in use to printed phone records issued by court order to police.

Firestone was standing close enough to Angelique's software for the program to pick up on his call from Toller and because Angelique was simultaneously examining the police printed records of the Brenner case and because Toller called Firestone with Sarah Brenner's phone, which was on the records, Angelique suspected Toller's guilt.

Chapter 9

If Angelique had been able to relay her suspicions of Toller to Firestone as immediately as she wanted, Firestone would have been able to make his arrests and wrap up his entire investigation within the hour, but that was not to be.

As Firestone pulled up in front of the Smith's quaint green tutor style home in its quiet family-friendly neighbourhood where the city met the suburbs, he realized that he'd forgotten the files that he had asked Angelique to print out for Daniel on her desk in his haste to meet Toller.

Firestone wrongfully assumed that she was calling him to point out his forgetfulness, so he could turn around, get his files, and save himself some travel time, but the prospect of spending more time with Toller was angering and stressful to him. He worried that, in his state, he would be insensitive to Angelique and he would then have more regrets on his mind due to his rudeness. In a mistaken effort to save himself some stress, he turned his phone off without speaking to Angelique.

As he walked to the door, Toller met him on the steps and eagerly jumped to her own defense.

"I simply tried to question her about her signatures on the lab reports we doubt. Suddenly, her husband rushes me and forces me out. I intended to arrest him for obstruction, but now a deadbolt is between him and I..."

Firestone strode right passed her angrily, knocked, and pressed his black and gold private investigator's card on to a glass feature beside the door.

Soon, they could hear footsteps approaching them and as the person walked, Firestone said, "Something tells me that these are not the first people to have a bad reaction to your particular brand of charm and trust me, I learned when I thought Mrs. Corrocco and her lawyer were being obstructive during my famous Carlton Tower investigation, emotion does not equal criminality under the law."

A burly gentleman with bushy orange hair on his head and face as well as heavy bags under his green eyes propped open the door. The man grumbled, "If you're with her, you can leave too. My wife and I can't answer your questions and we're prepared to sue for harassment if you choose not to believe us..."

As he began to close the door, Firestone speedily explained, "Mr. Smith, I realize that this is an inconvenient time for you and your wife to be questioned like this, but I need you to understand that your wife isn't under suspicion right now, but that can change and the questions will only get tougher from there."

Firestone's sincerity must have reached the man because he let them in, shook hands with them both, and introduced himself to them both apologetically as *Teddy.*

Upon entering, Firestone's nose was immediately burned by the smells of week-old garbage, cat, dog, and just a hint of artificially floral air freshener. The hallway leading into the home was packed, floor to ceiling, with fully stuffed garbage bags. There was only a narrow path through the trash.

As they walked the path, Firestone noted four cats precariously perched among the garbage, meowing in anger. Despite the cats, Firestone noticed rat droppings at his feet and he saw movement amid the garbage that he suspected was too small to be another cat. He could also hear a large dog barking from a room he could not see the doorway into through the trash. Firestone found himself wondering how the Smith's managed to keep so many animals alive.

Because of his broad build, Firestone had to walk in at an angle. Mr. Smith noticed that and apologized, saying, "I'm sorry about the mess. My wife and I have been spending quite a bit of time at the hospital lately. We lost our baby recently and my wife's recovery has been... complicated."

Firestone nodded sympathetically, but Toller kept her face crumpled in disgust.

After about five minutes of navigating the garbage maze, the group emerged in a sitting room that was considerably cleaner, which didn't mean much. Forensic Lab Nightshift Supervisor Tiffany Smith was waiting there for them.

The only way Tiffany Smith could have looked more like a zombie was if her crisp white nightdress was tattered, her hair was messier, and she started waddling towards them asking for their brains. She was tiny and she had a beautiful blonde braid with auburn undertones running down the front of her left shoulder. Her features struck Firestone as fairy-like, but she looked dead.

Her hair was crowning her extraordinarily pale and bruised face. Her green eyes were sunken into a raccoon mask of bags and bruises. Her expression was one of someone that had nothing else to live for.

For a millisecond, Firestone felt like leaving these broken people in peace, but then he remembered Toller had questions and she lacked the compassion to uncover the answers she needed another way, so he settled into the sitting room.

The sitting room had grey walls. There was a stained grey sofa and an eclectic mix of white chairs gathered around a very ornate coffee table. Each of the chairs had a rainbow array of decorative pillows that were so coated in pet hair that a person could not distinguish the pattern on them.

Toller made what Firestone thought was a mistake by settling onto the sofa. Although she quickly pushed the hair-covered pillows as far away from her as her arms could reach, Firestone could see even more stains bubble up from the couch as Toller's weight compressed the cushions. The longer he was in there, the harder it was to conceal his disgust, so he jumped immediately into questioning as he shoed a cat off of one of the white plastic chairs and sat.

"Hello, Tiffany, I'm Special Investigator Anthony Firestone and I'm here to ask you some questions... I'm afraid I don't know what Detective Toller already discussed with you before I arrived, so I may repeat some things..."

"To say that she *discussed* things with us is an insult to intellectuals everywhere, Mr. Firestone..." Teddy Smith asserted.

"I understand that," Firestone said genuinely, "And I'm sorry you were offended, but these questions we have are important."

Tiffany Smith nodded understandingly and Firestone went on, "We're here investigating some flawed reports coming out of the forensics lab where you work, Mrs. Smith." As soon as Firestone finished, the cat he had kicked off his chair jumped up on him and eventually fell asleep purring on his lap, prompting everyone, including Toller, to chuckle.

Despite the cat making moving difficult, Firestone showed her his file and asked, "Are these your signatures here?"

Tiffany raised her eyebrows; "It looks very similar, but it can't be. I was hospitalized when these were signed."

"Can you give us some proof of that?" Toller snarled.

Toller knew that at any moment, Teddy would step in and sabotage Tiffany's version of events because that was what she and Teddy had planned.

"I don't know. We must have a bill around here somewhere..."

She started to get up, but her husband apologetically stopped her, "I'm pretty sure we paid on the early bills, love. If we *do* have any receipts, it will take us hours to find them in this mess..."

"Oh I... I guess I can't prove it... right now... I mean."

"What hospital did you go to?" Firestone asked

"Mercy General..." her husband said hopefully. "Do you think that you can find it out for yourself?" As Teddy answered, a sly smile crept across Toller's lips.

As Firestone nodded, Mrs. Smith mumbled, "Really; I thought it was Saint Michaels." They could all tell she was fading fast.

Mr. Smith began to pull the brakes on the interview. "You were pretty out of it at the time dear, and now I can see that you need to lie down again."

"What doctor did you see?" Firestone pushed.

"His name was doctor Valley, like the type of field..." she said, "I'll never forget the man who told me I wasn't going to be a mother anymore."

There was a long moment of solemn silence as she started to get up to disappear.

"Just one more question, miss..." Firestone said as he stood to politely see her off.

"Yes?"

"As a supervisor, you must know the nightshift crew at the lab pretty well. Does anyone stand out to you as having the potential to forge your signature on error-filled reports?"

"That sounds like someone purposefully tried to sabotage my career..." Tiffany whispered incoherently.

"I'm afraid that is what this case is looking like..." Firestone said gently.

"Um," Mrs. Smith began to wobble; between the fatigue from her illness and the darkness of Firestone's questioning, she really was not doing well. Firestone and her husband steadied her as she finished, "As with any work place, there are some employees that work harder than others, but I don't believe even the worst of them would do this... I'm sorry, but I need to lie down."

"Of course," Firestone said with an appreciative nod. Tiffany Smith went further into the house for her nap and her husband went to tend to her, so Firestone and Toller left.

As soon as they were outside again, Toller resumed her badgering. "What was that supposed to be?"

"Questioning..." Firestone mumbled as his tired eyes rolled.

"They gave us nothing."

Firestone stopped and turned to her in a sudden snap of anger, "What did you expect them to say, Amanda? *Yes officers, it was me. I expected to fool you even though I signed my own name.* Besides, her sickness seems very real. I believe she was framed, but why and by who are going to be tough to answer."

"Oh, yeah, so where's our starting line? Like you said, she's obviously ill, possibly delirious, and her husband contradicted nearly everything she said. What do we believe enough to fact-check?"

"I don't know yet..."

They then resumed walking down to their cars. As they walked, Toller said, "I have something else for you to see in my car."

A chilling feeling suddenly washed over Firestone. Toller's tone was even colder than usual. *She had something bad to tell him.*

At her blue sedan, she showed Firestone a file and explained, "This is my printout from the department's cyber investigator. It shows that your boy, Dawson Sour, was not in France as he claimed. He was working overtime in place of Tiffany Smith. He's our man; we need to arrest him."

Firestone was struck with disbelief, but it was all there. A timesheet from the lab verified Sour's overtime. A passport tracking sheet also verified that Sour hadn't crossed a border recently and the airline verified Sour had booked a trip but cancelled at the last minute. Firestone had to admit that Sour needed to be taken in, at least for questioning.

Toller suddenly turned respectful. She touched his shoulder compassionately as she explained, "You can keep that folder for yourself; I have all of the necessary copies for evidence..."

Firestone sent Toller to make the arrest while he headed back to the law office to get Daniel's help in getting Sour a lawyer.

When Firestone made it to Daniel's office, however, he stumbled onto Daniel having a concerning fight with Leah.

Firestone heard Daniel hiss, "This has gone too far; you need to tell Anthony."

Leah looked like a threatened woman. She was tearful once again and desperately shaking her head, so Firestone stepped in, intending to help her. "You need to tell Anthony what?"

Leah stared at him for a long moment as Daniel stepped away. Suddenly, the same lifelessness that Firestone had seen in Tiffany Smith fell over Leah.

Leah finally said, "I have been having an affair."

Chapter 10

They both decided that it would not be wise to have such an emotional discussion in the office, so Firestone and Leah marched out together. Firestone eventually sat on a bench overlooking an outdoor art display about three blocks away from their office.

The display was an eclectic collection of decoratively sculptured water fountains that were as big as houses.

Firestone found himself looking up into the starlight and the glow of a crescent moon. It amazed him how fast the day had passed him by and how much his life had changed in such a short time.

As the calm cold of the night fell upon him, felt the irony of hearing his marriage was just about over in a romantic place like this; where so many proposals and marriage ceremonies took place.

Leah was too nervous to sit with him and take in the scenery as she explained, "Garth was my physical therapist following our shooting. He helped me heal on a different level than you did and he helped me find my psychiatrist."

Her words slowed. "As things went along, we started going for coffee, then dancing, then movies, and then hotel dates."

Firestone's head dropped. Her words meant that Leah had been in relationship with Garth since before their wedding. Had he known, he would have postponed the wedding, at least until Leah had a better idea of what and who she really wanted and if it turned out that what she really wanted was actually Garth, he would have backed off gracefully.

She droned on for a few more minutes about how great Garth was, how she didn't know who she was anymore, and how sorry she was because he was great too.

When he tuned back in, he heard, "Garth's been needling me for about six months now to talk to you. He wants to see if we can really make a go of things. He wants to marry me..."

"I was on the phone with Garth when you returned to the office this morning. I was crying because what Garth was saying was so sweet and his sweetness is part of what makes this whole thing so difficult. I love you, but I *need* him."

Firestone was petrified by a torrent of mixed emotions and when he failed to react, she went on to fill the silence, "He has two beautiful children and I want to be with them all, but you..."

Suddenly, Leah's entire demeanor shifted. She was still emotional for obvious reasons, but her posture and the lines in her face straightened. For a brief moment, he saw the strong-headed Leah he loved and missed so much.

She said, "You were the first man I ever truly loved. You loved me through heaven and hell and I owe you for that. I am your wife, so I want you to ask me to stay... or at least, say *something*."

After a while, her nerves bubbled over and she reverted back to being a lost woman. She begged him again to look at her and say something, but for the longest moment, he felt like he couldn't move. *What should he say?*

Amazingly enough, he didn't want to spit anger at her and he didn't feel sad. He was just tired of fighting a fight he now realized that he would never win.

He suddenly remembered their recent embrace in their rain soaked kitchen and how there was no love in it. He really recognized how much they both had changed and fallen apart.

She was not the Special Agent Leah Fong he had kicked down dozens of doors with or stood beside in firefights. She was no longer the version of herself that refused to let him give up. She was a broken woman who, for months, had been asking without asking for him to let her go.

He then turned their entire relationship over in his mind. He realized that they had always been *partners:* more than friends, but not exactly lovers. He found himself questioning whether their marriage had ever been a marriage at all or whether it was just what happened when they both woke up in the hospital after their shooting and found out they had lost too much already to lose that connection to each other also.

He finally looked up at her because he knew what he had to say. He then took a deep breath and asked, "Does he make you happy?"

He surprised her when he walked up and wrapped her in his arms as she answered, "Yes..." Firestone could feel that Leah wanted to elaborate but she stopped herself in a slow effort to spare his feelings.

Firestone loved Leah more than life itself. The prospect of her no longer being his wife, his best friend, and his partner was heartbreaking. He couldn't stop his tears and his voice cracked, but he famed a smile, pulled her closer, and said what he needed to say:

"As badly as I want you to stay; I think you'd better go because you're not in love with me." The tone of his words told Leah what was really in his heart.

Leah blinked with more surprise. In that instant, they both came to same realization: Leah never understood how deeply Firestone really loved her.

Leah squeezed him tighter as her mind began to change, but Firestone accepted that they could never really be happy together if she was only competing with his affection out of guilt instead of letting what was really in her heart flow freely, so he began to pull away.

When some distance developed between them, he leaned in and kissed her mouth. When they broke apart once more, he said, "I love you Leah Fong, but I don't have the strength to keep fighting for you."

He stepped back further, "All I've ever wanted is for you be happy. If he does that for you, then I wish the best for you both and I think you'll be a great mom."

Leah realized he was right and shook her head in regret as he called back to her, "I'll call you once I get settled in a new apartment, so I can pick my stuff up when it's not awkward and I'll resign from the firm as soon as possible..."

Firestone could hear Leah sobbing and it took every ounce of Firestone's strength to leave her as she cried, but he knew that he had to because the decision to stay with him had to be from her heart and no because of his influence.

From the distance he had now walked from her, he called back, "Leah, I love you, so I can't keep you down. Do what will make you happy in the long run and not what you think I want. We'll both survive this, no matter what you decide..."

With that, Firestone walked away from the only thing in the world that really mattered to him.

PART THREE – THE TRUTH HURTS

Chapter 11

Hours later, a knock at his door pulled Firestone out of bed.

He opened the door to see a bike messenger holding two legal envelopes. "Are you Anthony Firestone?" he whispered.

"Yes."

The messenger handed Firestone the envelopes and a clipboard, saying, "I'm sorry for the early hour sir, but this was marked urgent... I need to see some ID and then I need you to sign this form verifying that you received it."

Firestone did as the manager asked and the man left Firestone with his envelope.

Although it was early, the messenger hadn't woken Firestone up. Torturous memory flashes of Leah's smile, her laugh, and that grateful embrace when she was rescued from the Golden Dragons' keep kept Firestone awake.

Since Leah's admission of her affair earlier that night, Firestone had settled in to a hotel room a floor down from the one he had rented with Leah. Until the messenger had arrived, Firestone was annoyed by the fact that his room was basically completely white and therefore offered no distraction from his thoughts of Leah while he tossed and turned, alone and awake in bed. The envelopes offered that much-needed distraction.

He set the envelopes down on the desk and began processing their contents.

The first envelope held divorce papers from Leah, delivered courtesy of Daniel's law office. He knew that they meant Leah had made her final decision; she had chosen Garth.

As bad as that fact hurt him, he was grateful that particular emotional roller coaster ride was over. He finalized things for himself by signing the papers right away. He kept his half of the agreed-upon potential sale price of their house once the renovation was finished, his pension from the FBI, his half of their mutual savings account, and his car.

Leah had an expansive estate because her family had always been accomplished. Daniel immigrated to America more than a decade before Leah and the rest of their family made the trip. Leah's parents and other siblings died on the boat ride over, but Leah's parents left their farm back in China to Daniel before traveling.

Daniel renovated the farm into an exclusive vacationer's bed and breakfast over the years and between the money that brought in and her equal shares of Daniel's firm and estate, Firestone could have easily leached for a lot more money, but he refused to let himself feel entitled to what he didn't earn.

The second envelope contained the cases he had asked Angelique to finalize for the law firm, but forgot on her desk.

Firestone was about to return to his tossing and turning when his cell phone started to ring. It was Angelique and she was trying to make a video call. He pulled on a sleeveless shirt and answered.

"Tony, are you alright? I just got off the phone with Leah. She told me that she left you. *She left you; that bitch must be crazy.*"

Firestone laughed tearfully, "I think I'll make it. Thanks for the support and the files, all the same."

"I couldn't sleep after Leah gave me the news, so I finished that additional research you asked for. I was able to find copies of Tanning's file for

Brenner deep in his firm's servers. Everything looks above board there."

"So why did Tanning have the only copy?" Firestone asked.

"I found some emails between a forensic scientist and a new associate at Tanning's office. The scientist convinced Tanning's underling that the file Tanning received was a mistake and the underling deleted it. The same scientist that reached out to Tanning's office also submitted the report that the prosecution received..."

"Ok, so there was a police cover up, orchestrated by Sour. The police have him in custody now and they will uncover why he did it, but tell me, was someone trying to sabotage Brenner or Tanning?"

Angelique laughed, "Tony, Sour was in France when the forensics were contaminated. I've already passed the proof of that discreetly onto a clean detective in charge of investigating him. Your new partner is the one responsible for the cover up and she framed Sour for it."

Firestone was surprised and confused, "But how... my partner had paperwork from the police department. Are you certain she's not the one being framed?"

"Positive," Angelique asserted, "First, the file I composed is incredibly extensive because Tanning was a lawyer for 29 years. In that time, he made some enemies, but it appears that he always followed the law to letter; meaning that his clients were always satisfied and none of his opponents had the drive to kill him, but it took time to verify all that *and* prove that none of those potential enemies were in that courthouse themselves or paid someone in there."

"Because Tanning's killer had to be in the courthouse to be able to dose Tanning's food..." Firestone clarified.

"Exactly," Angelique said with an enthusiastic jump, "I also had to do similar searches on the people in Brenner's life. Even with my immense computing power and help from various sources, to do a search like that, even just on Sour, takes a lot of time; more time than your partner applied to making her file."

"Once I was satisfied that Tanning wasn't a central target, I had to look into Brenner and the lawyers Brenner supposedly killed. I compiled a list of who'd want to see those lawyers dead. I then compiled a list of who would want to see Brenner jailed and cross-referenced both lists."

"I uncovered that the murdered lawyers had records similar to Tanning's *with no one angry enough to kill them*, but *Sarah Brenner* would *benefit* from Daily's death *and* Landon's arrest..."

"How so..."

"With Daily's death, the Brenner's divorce is stalled and whatever divorce arrangements were previously made would be invalidated. If Landon is convicted of murder, Sarah stands to take him for everything he has and he couldn't fight her..."

"Oh that's clever," Firestone said, "But how did Toller and the rest of the police get dragged into the scheme?"

"I don't know that exactly, but, when you arrived, I was running a cell phone call tracing program I am trying to develop. When that call from your partner came in, you were standing close enough to my computer for the software to pick up your call. Initially, I dismissed it, but since then, my computer matched the number that called you to the one that texted Brenner to be in the park..."

"Ok…"

"A full explanation of my number tracking technology is quite technical and proprietary, but Tony, your partner Toller was using Sarah Brenner's phone when she called you. I know that for a fact and I also that, for your partner to be using her phone, Toller must know Sarah Brenner…"

"Well, thank-you, Angelique; I think I'd better hang up and go deal with this…"

"Good luck." Angelique hung up.

Firestone paced the room for a long moment, suddenly he recognized how much his current predicament reminded him of his famed Carlton Tower Investigation.

Both investigations had criminals that seemed to have insider knowledge that kept them just out of Firestone's reach. Both investigations were hindered by his worrying about Leah and both cases featured sickly women that had key stories to tell; in the Carlton Tower case, it was Elise Corrocco, but now it was Tiffany Smith.

Ever since his visit to the Smith's, Firestone was unable to shake the feeling that Tiffany knew more than she claimed. After all, why was her name used on the forged reports? Involving her in this scandal the way the report writer did would likely cost her career; who hated such a soft person enough to do that to her? Did she really not know who hated her that deeply?

Firestone then remembered that like the Carlton Tower's Elise Corrocco, Tiffany Smith was kept from telling Firestone everything that she knew by both her illness and a caring man that wanted to protect her.

Then he remembered, Elise Corrocco was guilty and her protective lawyer was complicit. What first looked like a terrorist strike was actually an elaborate cover up of a fragile woman's bitterness. Nothing was what it seemed to be; maybe this case was equally as deceiving.

Firestone quickly settled into the desk and began pouring over Angelique's findings and comparing them to what Toller had found.

Soon, he came to a sickening conclusion but he found himself smiling and nodding along because he had to ask himself: *'Could it really be that simple?'*

He had to make nearly a dozen phone calls to be sure.

Chapter 12

Only two hours later, Firestone was up, dressed for work, and speeding down a highway. His siren was sounding, his emergency lights were aglow, and he had several patrol cars on his bumper. They were all racing to the Smith house, believing that their purpose was a matter of life or death.

Firestone soon booted down the doorway, plowed through the trashy maze to the bedroom, and immediately handcuffed a terrified Tiffany Smith. Teddy Smith protested violently but Firestone ultimately fought him off and one of the uniformed officers quickly hauled Teddy away.

Once the Smith's were in custody, Firestone called Toller.

Toller walked in expecting to help Firestone interrogate the Smiths. True to that form, Firestone was already seated and all set up for the interrogation with files all laid out, snacks, and water in front of him and a camera on a tripod ready to film the discussion, but he was alone in the room.

She set herself up and asked, "Who's first: Mr. or Mrs. Smith?"

"Neither one; this is me interrogating you…" He said.

Toller's faked innocence was Oscar worthy, "Me?! Have you lost your mind?"

Firestone kept his voice soft and unwavering. His quiet confidence convinced her to sit in the suspect's chair as he said, "My mind's fine; thanks for asking. I went to my friend the computer expert, even though you advised me not to, and she confirmed for me, even before combing through your laptop, that you are, indeed, guilty…"

"You killed Fred Tanning and orchestrated an incredibly overcomplicated cover up intended to obscure the truth about who killed Lawrence Daily."

"You *are* crazy! That quote-unquote expert of yours needs to be added to our list of suspects. I don't even know a Lawrence Daily…" Toller grumbled.

Firestone agreed, explaining, "Well, he *was* Landon Brenner's divorce attorney, but you didn't have to know Daily. Who he was wasn't as important as the fact that he was the person most likely for Landon Brenner to murder because they'd fought the day of Daily's murder and Daily had, in his attaché case, *falsified* documents implicating Brenner in an identity theft scheme. Apparently, Daily was desperate to be rid of Brenner that he was willing to openly ruin Brenner's career if Brenner refused to let him quit *and* it wasn't your job to kill *him.*"

"You merely aided the person who did kill Daily by using your position in Internal Affairs to blackmail Officer Ron Michaels and a few forensics people with their career failings that only IA knows about. You blackmailed those people into ensuring that Landon Brenner was arrested, tried, and convicted for Daily's murder. Tanning stood between you and Brenner's conviction, so you killed him..."

"All I don't know about the Daily, Brenner, and Tanning situation is why you got involved with them at all. Based on what I've found, your original murderous motives were quite different..."

Firestone remained immovable as he continued to explain, "The thing that bothered me the most about this case was Tiffany Smith. When we interviewed her, she seemed so innocent and sweet that I struggled to understand why someone would want to tangle her up in this scandal and when I asked Sour about it, he confirmed that Tiffany was as beloved as she appeared to be. Then, my own wife informed me that she was leaving me for another man and my perspective changed."

"I realized how easy it is to assume that someone love loves you just as much as you love them just because you're married. I failed to see her slipping away. I failed to see the disrespect brewing in my own wife and I wondered if Tiffany was missing the same signs in her husband. I then had the sickening thought that, if your marriage is ending, the last thing you want is to have a baby; maybe Tiffany's miscarriage was not so natural..."

"I phoned the two hospitals the Smith's mentioned during their interview, Mercy General and Saint Michaels, and I found Doctor Valley, at Saint Michaels not Mercy General Hospital by the way. He verified that he'd been treating Tiffany Smith since *long before* the Brenner car crash. She *was* in hospital when her name was signed on the damaging reports."

"I explained my concerns to him and he re-examined Tiffany's medical records and samples with my concerns in mind. Doctor Valley eventually confirmed that Tiffany Smith's blood was near-saturated with potentially fatal levels of Zinc Phosphide and Salicylate; that combination is common chemical blend in rat poison. Valley said that Tiffany Smith miscarried because of those chemicals are such powerful blood-thinners that a fetus couldn't hold together and Tiffany's body couldn't recover after the miscarriage because she simply continued to bleed."

"I staged Tiffany Smith's arrest, so she could get the proper medical treatment without her husband there, ready to finish the job. I eventually confronted Teddy Smith, he realized he was caught, and accepted a deal."

Toller's lowered her head until it touched the table.

Firestone could now see the curtain closing on her innocent act, but he continued, "As part of his deal, he pointed us to the cheating spouses website the two of you found one another through. My friend, the computer expert that you recommended I avoid, uncovered the messages between you two where you detail how killing Tiffany with poison would look more like a pregnancy gone wrong than murder."

Firestone then walked over and pulled up the blinds that showed Teddy Smith in the next interrogation room. He was writing a statement before two other detectives. Showing Toller Teddy was a wordless reminder that she was doomed.

Firestone respectfully dropped his voice and head as he explained, "Teddy admitted that he created the mess in their home to attract vermin, so he could buy poison, and dose Tiffany's food and drinks with it."

"I recognize that your plan went like this: you fell into a relationship with Teddy Smith, Tiffany Smith's husband, but Tiffany was already pregnant and you knew a divorce wasn't to be clean, so you two, Teddy and you, conspired to kill her in a way that looked like natural causes, but what I don't know, and what your saving grace might be, is why mix Tiffany and the Brenner case together?"

Toller lifted her head. Firestone could see that she was tearful yet hopeful as he had mentioned a saving grace.

He continued more slowly, hoping she'd jump in and give him some answers. "Teddy Smith also told us that you needed someone within the crime lab that you could blame for the holes in the Brenner case, so he gave you samples of Mrs. Smith's signature so that you could frame her, but you had to realize a supervisor's name on a basic report is abnormal, it immediately draws attention..."

It didn't take him more than those few sentences to recognize that, although there was a part of her wanted to speak in her own defence, Toller intended to remain tight-lipped, so he adjusted.

He sat down, looked her right in the eyes, and took her hand in his. He said, "Amanda, you need to talk to me. I know what you've done and I've got the paper to prove it."

He let go of her hand and began leafing through the papers he had in front of him. He started pushing papers in front of Toller and said, "Curiously enough, my expert ran all the same background, financial, and computer usage history checks that you claimed to have gotten from your own expert. Your version, here..." He pointed out one of the stacks of sheets he'd pushed in front of her, "Incriminates Dawson Sour in the cover up, however my experts findings," he pointed to another stack beside her version, "Verify that Sour was in France, as he claimed. Obviously, one of these reports is a fake."

"I considered that it could be my expert that was mistaken, but then, I noticed that my expert's file has pages of different sizes, color, thickness, and so on. Your 'expert's' file is too consistent. My computer expert was able to confirm that you typed this up yourself and printed it off at the library..."

"My expert also unearthed the file Tanning had in court. Someone at Tanning's firm deleted it and shredded all paper copies after Tanning took his copy to court."

"Someone from the forensics lab reached out to them and lied that the reports were flawed. Luckily, it's very hard to actually delete something and it's even harder to replace the real thing with speedily composed forgeries..."

Firestone paused for a sip of water before he continued, "My expert, Angelique, tracked down the forensic scientist that reached out to Tanning's firm. Under pressure from a very angry Prosecutor Lang, the man confirmed that the order to do the deletions ultimately came from you..."

He took her hand again, "Amanda, when what my expert found is combined with Teddy Smith's statement and Doctor Valley's testimony, you'll be charged and likely convicted of obstruction of justice, racketeering, and conspiracy to murder. Once convicted, you'll be a woman who is a cop and is headed for prison; likely for life…"

Amanda Toller may as well have been encased in marble. She didn't move or make a sound.

Firestone pushed, "Amanda, we already know that you sabotaged the forensic reports in the Brenner file and we also confirmed your number is the number Tanning found on Brenner's phone, luring him to the park. We know you're involved, but if you can explain why, I can help you."

Finally, Toller broke, "My connection to Brenner is quite sorted. I want some security in writing. I want a lawyer and a sit down with an assistant district attorney before I say anything more."

It only took a matter of seconds for Prosecutor Lang and a court-appointed attorney to join them in the room because they were already in the building making deals with Teddy Smith and others.

Toller was soon covered under a fine plea agreement and started talking again, "Sarah Brenner is a personal friend of mine." She said slowly, "Because of Landon Brenner's internet success, Sarah Brenner's professional success gets lost, but she's a gynecologist and obstetrician." Toller spoke like that was all she needed to say, but no one else made any connection.

Toller sighed in frustration and went on, "She was Tiffany Smith's doctor. She suspected that Tiffany was being poisoned and came to me because she knew I was a police officer."

"I felt forced to tell her that Tiffany's husband was poisoning her for me. I expected her to turn me in, but instead, she asked me for help framing Landon for murder. She promised that she'd bury my involvement in Tiffany Smith's murder and give me half of the Brenner estate so Teddy Smith and I could start over."

"I had no idea what she was planning; I just had to wait for her call."

"Like Firestone said, as an officer at Internal Affairs, I had that second-rate boob Officer Michaels and a few forensic investigators under my thumb. Through them, things happened pretty much exactly like how Tanning alluded to in court."

"Sarah lured a drunk Landon out to that pond after she crashed into those lawyers and sunk the car. Apparently, he walked in on his own and soaked himself in pond water, trying to save his car."

"The officers that I owned stacked the decks against Brenner. They ignored Sarah's accident-induced injuries and falsified reports and everything was going our way until Brenner hired Tanning."

"I didn't own every investigator that looked at Brenner's car, so a real report was made. Tanning must've printed his file before the people I owned could erase it because he was so damn efficient."

"Initially, Sarah tried to buy Tanning off because the man had a sleazy reputation, but it turned out to be just talk. Apparently, Tanning never gave or took a bribe in his life and he wasn't willing to change for us, but he was unbelievably cocky…"

"Tanning may as well have been attaching us to the wall with a power drill in court that day. Because we'd attempted to bribe him, Tanning knew we were guilty and he used that knowledge to manipulate the jury into freeing Landon Brenner and convicting us legally. His every word screwed us into a corner tighter and tighter because it made everyone suspicious of us, but suspicion is one thing; proof is another thing.

"If his claims had been substantiated, he would have blown down the whole house of cards. I felt I had no choice. I induced my own allergic reaction to strawberries, took all of Tanning's medication and I soaked his meal with peanut oil while I choked. Even with medication which I made sure he didn't have access to, the man was dead after the first forkful."

Toller watched the reflection of her fidgeting fingers in the surface of the scarred stainless-steel interrogation table as she said, "What I hadn't considered was that Tanning managed to talk to Judge Harmon before eating."

She then looked straight into Firestone's eyes. "The next thing I knew, I was face to face with you. I thought I could handle you, but we can all see how that turned out."

Firestone leaned in, "You are not the first to underestimate me and you're not going to be the last. You have your golden plea deal, now where is Sarah Brenner?"

"I don't know. I wouldn't be surprised if she's already left the country; after all, she has Brenner's money run with... I met with her to explain how complicated things had gotten before I met you at the Smith's. We must've switched phones accidently at that meeting because this one is *hers.* That's why your computer expert matched it to the text luring Brenner to the park when Sarah did the luring..."

Firestone took the phone and blasted out of the interrogation room and immediately got in touch with two people using it: Judge Harmon and Brenner's estate's attorney. Both verified that Brenner's estate had been virtually completely liquefied by Sarah Brenner since the night Lawrence Daily and his associates were killed by the car.

Both men also verified that a flight plan had been filed for Brenner's private jet. In less than three hours, Sarah Brenner would successfully escape with Landon's private jet and fortune to Belize. If she made it there, there would be no way to make her face justice for her involvement in the murders and cover up.

Chapter 13

Firestone found himself experiencing Déjà vu. Seven years ago: he was in a similar unmarked federal SUV, racing down this same highway, heading for the same airfield he was presently headed for, and he was once again headed to stop his murder suspect from boarding a private jet. Back then, his suspects in the Carlton Tower investigation escaped; he was determined not to have that happen twice.

Meanwhile, up the road and at the private jet, Sarah Brenner was speedily transferring her suitcases from the back of her hatchback SUV onto the plane. Although, at that point, she didn't realize how close she was to being arrested, she recognized that her packing up was taking too long. She was getting anxious and embittered towards her driver and the flight crew that were trying to help her.

"You idiots!" She shouted, "This is Marie Belswap designer luggage. It's $2000 a suitcase and you're scuffing it."

While she shouted, Firestone and some other officers pulled in. Seven years ago, Firestone was kept from his suspects by a fence, but, thanks to Judge Harmon calling ahead, that fence was opened for Firestone.

Seeing the police approach made Sarah flinch and dash for the plane, but her flight crew had many more scruples than Firestone's previous suspect's had. The honorable crew shut everything down, leaving Sarah nowhere to run. Because she had no other option, Sarah submitted to being arrested relatively calmly.

PART FOUR – AS THE STORM BLOWS OVER

Chapter 14

After a decent night's sleep, a couple of healthy meals, and a few hot showers; Firestone and Daniel were enjoying Chinese takeout in Daniel's office while Firestone explained what had happened during his private project for Judge Harmon.

"Sarah Brenner gave a detailed confession." Firestone exclaimed, "She explained that she wanted to kill her husband for a long time because she had grown tired of his playboy lifestyle and inescapable shadow."

"She considered it, but felt divorce wasn't enough to get her out. Landon then called her and professed his undying love for her as well as his agreement that their divorce was a mistake. He detailed the argument he'd had with his lawyer, Lawrence Daily, and asked her to meet him in the park for a second marriage proposal."

"Apparently, Sarah became undecided about her love for Landon, but she ultimately loved the idea of having all of his money to herself more; remember, the woman was willing to allow her pregnant patient, Tiffany Smith, to be murdered in exchange for help disguising her own guilt, so a loving heart was never her strongest feature."

Daniel nodded and Firestone went on, "Her confliction convinced her to send Landon to prison instead of killing him. Getting Landon convicted and having Daily dead got her the fortune just the same as Landon's death would."

Daniel nodded more. Firestone continued on, "She invited Landon over to keep him good and drunk while she had access to his car and then she simply called the law firm and found out that Lawrence Daily had gone to Crooks Bar that night."

"She confirmed Daily was there, waited, and then ran him down with Landon's car when he came out. Sarah was bruised in the murderous accident, so she lied about Landon attacking her and she staged the scene at the park that spotlighted Landon as the murderer. My partner, Amanda Toller, took it from there."

"Sarah Brenner and Toller had a previous arrangement once Toller explained to Sarah why Tiffany Smith was so ill. Toller and her dirtied team waited in the wings until Sarah called and they corrupted the Brenner as much as they could for as long as they could."

"They probably would've succeeded if it wasn't for the fact that not every investigator at the scene was owned by her, so a real report was sent to Tanning. Toller tried to take it back, but Tanning was too efficient and Harmon was too honest for her to succeed. Toller is now facing 20 years in protective custody with an eligibility for parole in 10 years."

"Sarah's lawyer did arrange a plea deal, but as the actual murderer and the last in the conspiracy to speak up, she did not have a lot of leverage to negotiate with. She'll be serving 45 years with the potential for parole after 35 years."

"Ouch." Daniel said between chopstick swirls of noodles.

Firestone nodded, saying, "All of Landon Brenner's charges have been reduced to time served in custody, but, surprisingly enough, he has chosen to stand by Sarah. Apparently, they plan to continue their marriage and work on its flaws while Sarah is in prison..."

"Sour was also cleared of all wrong doing and has stepped in as Tiffany Smith's temporary replacement while she continues to heal in hospital. Tiffany and Teddy Smith are now divorcing and Teddy is facing a future of mental health help more so than prison."

"The officers that Toller was blackmailing have all been suspended, pending fair investigations into the matters that Toller held over them as well as investigations into how deeply they were involved in this new conspiracy. I don't know much, but I suspect none of them will do jail time."

Daniel chuckled and asserted, "And I saw Assistant District Attorney Lang's campaign speech on the TV earlier this afternoon. She was preaching about how she helped clean up the department and how she's going to transfer that cleanliness to the city, *especially if* she is elected DA."

Firestone smiled and nodded, "All in all, I'd say it's pretty great for only a few days work and I've finally placed those files that I owe you on your desk... I'm sorry I was so late on those, but with everything else..." Firestone shook his head in shame.

Daniel waved him off understandingly.

Firestone then placed some distance between him and the food. He then dried his sweaty palms on his pant legs for a moment and stated, "I can't stop talking for the same reason you can't seem to start; neither of us wants to discuss what happened between me and Leah or what that happening means for my career here, but I've already decided that it's best if I just step away. I think it's what's best for us both..."

Daniel cut him off, "I'm sorry, Anthony; I truly am. You see, I knew that Leah was dating Garth while she was engaged to you."

Firestone was both hurt and surprised by his brother-in-law's words, but he continued to listen as Daniel explained, "I trusted her to have the decency to choose one of you before committing to a marriage and when she didn't, I'd hoped she'd work it out with you, but she didn't."

"I understand you want to leave, but the bottom line is that I still need an investigator and you still need a job. I feel I owe you so I promise better pay and more freedom as far as hours go but..."

"Daniel, I can't watch Leah build a life with another man. My office is across from hers and the doors of both of our offices are glass and you are her brother; there is no escape from her here..."

"Just for a few months; until I can find another investigator..."

"How can I say no?" Firestone was legitimately asking for a way out, but Daniel made it clear with his expression that there was no way out.

That night, Firestone moved back into the apartment-style townhouse he'd lived in before he and Leah married.

The first thing he did was put his fist through his overly-colorful bedroom wall. At the start of this month, he had a wife, a nicer house, and a job that he enjoyed. Now, his wife was his ex-wife, his house was hers, and his job had become a prison.

He had to ask himself: how had he fallen so far; and what was next for him?

www.ingramcontent.com/pod-product-compliance
Lightning Source LLC
Chambersburg PA
CBHW052320220526
45472CB00001B/200